BC

Course, A. G.

Windjammers of the Horn: the story of the last British fleet of square-rigged sailing ships

Windjammers of the Horn

By the same author:

The Wheel's Kick and the Wind's Song
Ships of the P & O
The Merchant Navy Today
The Deep Sea Tramp
Painted Ports
Dictionary of Nautical Terms
The Merchant Navy: A Social History
Docks and Harbours of Britain
A Seventeenth Century Mariner
Pirates of the Eastern Seas

Captain A G Course

Windjammers of the Horn

The story of the last British fleet
of square-rigged sailing ships

Adlard Coles Ltd

First published in 1969 by Adlard Coles Limited
3 Upper James Street, Golden Square, London W1
Printed in Great Britain by
Ebenezer Baylis & Son, Limited
The Trinity Press, Worcester, and London
SBN: 229 98578 5

Dedicated to the scattered remnant of a vanished age

Contents

Appendices

Acknowledgements

Without the help of the good friends mentioned here this book could not have been written. Captain Sir J P Williams CMG OBE, Chairman of the Australian National Line of Steamships, contributed his experiences as 2nd Mate and 1st Mate in two of the windjammers and Mr Lionel Adams, Chairman of the Australian Canned Fruits Board, sent me his experiences in two others. Captain J D L Williams, Regional Controller of Shipping and Transport of Tasmania, and Captain E B Carter, late Marine Superintendent of the Colonial Sugar Refining Company, Australia, also served in the ships and gave me material for the book. Of the many others who helped are included:

Captains J W Broadhouse and J M Hood of New Zealand and Captain Frank Walker from Mississippi, USA.

In England help was sent in the form of MSS by Captains R E Clare, F W J Pearce and J A McBrearty, Cdr F A C Bishop, Lt Cdr B Penrose, Mr R M Sibun, Mr L W Rolfe, Mr G H G Dunne, Mr Stan Hugill and the late Captain E G Byrne. Everyone sent their experiences in the windjammers of the Marine Navigation Company, and to them, and others mentioned in the text, I give my thanks.

Over 200 photographs were sent to me for illustrations and, as is inevitable, the copies of some received had already been sent to me. I wish to thank the following for supplying those reproduced:

The National Maritime Museum for Nos 1, 2, 3, 4, 11; the late Nautical Photo Agency for 9, 10; Captain F W J Pearce for 14, 19, 20, 22; Mr L Adams for 5, 6, 8; Captain F Walker for 16, 17, 26; Mr L M Rolfe for 7, 12, 23; Captain J D L Williams for 15, 24; Lt Cdr B Penrose for 27, 28; Mr Thomson, son of the late Captain David Thomson, 18, 25; Mr S Hugill for 29, 30; Captain Sir J P Williams for 21; and Mr G H G Dunne for 13.

My special thanks are due to Derek G. M Gardner, FRSMA, for the picture of the *Garthpool* on the jacket and the sail plans at the end of the book.

Plates

to be found between pages 96 and 97

Introduction

Windjammer is a colloquialism for the last type of the square-rigged sailing ship. The name originated in the United States of America in 1899, and although British seamen disliked it they accepted it and the word came into common usage. When a square-rigged vessel was sailing as close to the wind as possible, her lower yards were braced sharp up to such an angle as to be almost touching the forward shrouds and rigging on the lee side of the ship. She was then said to be jammed hard-up into the wind. Hence windjammer!

As opposed to a clipper a windjammer was a full-lined ship, oblong and box-shaped under the waterline, and when loaded carried almost twice the amount of cargo as a fine-lined clipper of the same dimensions. Consequently, being that much heavier, she had to carry a large sail-area to drive her along at nearly the same speed. Her yards were longer and her sails wider and much heavier; and she was difficult and dangerous to handle in bad weather. To make it more hazardous the crews were reduced in the interests of economy, which was necessary to compete with steamships; for, to compensate for the longer passages and voyages, freight rates had to be reduced in the windjammers.

This is the story of the ships, barques and men of Sir William Garthwaite's Marine Navigation Company.

One of the first of his fleet was the three-masted barque *Carnmoney* of 1,255 tons net, which he bought from John Stewart and Company of London for £7,600 at Hull towards the end of 1915 when she was loading in Alexandra Dock for Bahia Blanca. John Stewart and Company and William Garthwaite were not the only windjammer owners in Great Britain to carry on after the first world war. Thomas Shute & Company of Liverpool did so with their *Tamar* until 1922, and it was about the same time that James Bell and Company Limited of Hull sold their last square-rigger. The latter shipowners had started in 1917 with the ship *Neotsfield*, 1,894 tons, which they bought from R Thomas & Company Limited of Liverpool. They bought some prize sailing ships captured during the First World War, and owned altogether six windjammers and changed their names, starting them with the prefix 'Bell'. They were all sold by 1922 or very soon after.

Late in 1915 Sir William bought the steel full-rigged ship *Queen Elizabeth*, 1,700 tons net, built in 1889. He never saw her for she was sunk soon after sailing from Liverpool on the 2nd December. During the war he also bought the *Invercauld*, *Invermay*, *Inverneill*, *Invergarry* and *Inversnaid*. The first two were sunk before he had time to change their names.

It has been said that the apprentices who received valuable training in the windjammers were regarded as cheap labour by the owners. They received no wages and there can be no doubt that the high premiums paid by their parents helped to make it possible to run the ships. Sir William issued instructions to his masters that the training of apprentices was a work of national importance and that particular care should be paid to their nautical education and their welfare. Whether this was possible can be decided after the stories of the voyages have been related. He also asked that a regular course of instruction be mapped out, supervised by the masters and put in charge of competent officers. I will record the instances, if any, where this was done, but, judging from my own experiences in windjammers, I have no hesitation in saying that rarely, if ever, was it carried out.

My instruction in John Stewart's ships and barques was aimed at making me a competent seaman in six months. We apprentices soon learned that we were there to make up any shortage of men in the fo'c'sle. As it became more difficult to get the services of efficiently trained sailing-ship men in the fo'c'sle so the number of apprentices was increased. Why did the men and lads go to sea in windjammers and endure so much discomfort besides the hazards encountered? It was said that the boys were too young to realise what they were letting themselves in for and the fo'c'sle hands arrived on board too drunk to know they had sailed. Exaggeration of course! Advice given by experienced officers and masters; knowledge that a sailing ship certificate would be looked on with favour by the more sought-after shipping companies; and, perhaps above all, reading stories of adventure in sailing ships, are the chief reasons for the choice of a sailing ship training by apprentices.

In the days of Sir William Garthwaite's fleet of windjammers many pilotage authorities insisted on sail training as a qualification. As late as

1919 the Blue Funnel Line demanded a square-rigged (sailing ship) master's certificate for entry into their Company as a junior officer. Naturally it was harder to get sail training in the last years of the windjammers.

'The Merchant Shipping Act of 1906' brought in an improved 'Scale of Provisions for Seamen'. The author enjoyed its benefits but can only say that he and his fellow apprentices found it insufficient, although we did not suffer in health because of the lack of quantity. One temptation we found hard to resist was to return a part of the meat, salt or tinned, served out to us for our midday meal, for making hash for our supper. If none was returned there was no evening meal and nothing more to eat, except weevily, hard Liverpool Pantiles (ship's biscuits) until breakfast time next morning.

Under the 1906 Act ships were allowed to load deeper. Whether it was a compensation to shipowners for the extra cost of supplying standard provisions the author does not know. The average increase in draught for sailing ships was three inches which gave an increase of about 100 tons in cargo-carrying capacity. It was a cruel and murderous thing to do, for sailing ships were already loaded deeply enough and were taking such heavy seas on deck that many were lost, with their crews, especially off Cape Horn. The yearly average of deaths in the windjammers, even in their then depleted numbers was 698 casualties to ships and from accidents, 505. The freeboard—distance from the load line to the main (working deck) in the author's barques—was only four feet six inches; in the smaller barques owned by Sir William Garthwaite it was only four feet four and a half inches. In every gale, in loaded barques and ships, heavy seas swept the decks fore and aft. Seamen and officers alike were in danger of being washed overboard and drowned or badly injured and, in spite of oilskins and seaboots, were always wet through.

What was the reaction of the sailing ship apprentices to his initiation to the life at sea in the windjammer? It was frightening and much more hazardous than he had imagined. Climbing the rigging when the windjammer was moored in the still waters of a dock was not difficult, but when she was rolling and pitching in a heavy sea it became dangerous.

Climbing over the fore, main and mizzen tops, and the crosstrees, was frightening at first. One had to incline backwards at an angle of forty-five degrees to climb the rope ladder, and that at a height of fifty or a hundred feet above the deck. The more attractive and safer method was to climb up through and inside of the rope ladder, but this took longer and was so much despised by seamen that this way up was known as 'through the lubbers' hole'.

The rope ladders of the rigging finished some twenty or thirty feet from the top of the masts and to reach the royal yard, when hoisted, a wire rope had to be climbed by the hand-over-hand method with no foothold. One of the most difficult and hazardous operations that I experienced as a rather small boy of fifteen was getting from the weather rigging—one always had to climb up on the weather side so that the wind would blow one towards the rigging and not away from it—on to the footrope of the lower yards. When the yards were braced up sharply there was a big gap here and one needed long legs to span it. I had to give what almost amounted to a jump to get hold of the jackstay or hand-rail on top of the yard and land on my feet on the footrope underneath the yard.

Then there was the first experience of a sea crashing over the bulwarks on to the main deck. When hauling on the braces, which swung the yards round, or the ropes used in setting or hauling up the sails, one could not let go and make a rush to hang on to the lifeline. It sometimes happened that one or more of the seamen was washed away along the deck, and sometimes washed overboard or at least injured. The hazards in sailing ships are dealt with more fully later with accounts of actual happenings.

Few sailing ship apprentices were taught navigation on board, and, in the author's experience and knowledge, had to learn what they could from navigation books with no help. Certainly no practical experience was obtainable. The only member of the crew on board besides the master who was allowed to do any practical navigation was the first mate. It is true that there were good navigators in the windjammers but most of them got by with an altitude of the sun about eight o'clock in the morning to work out the longitude, and another at noon to determine the latitude.

If there was no sun to observe then an approximate position was obtained by dead reckoning which included the distance run, the true course steered and an allowance for leeway, tides or currents. Stars were not used for sextant altitudes, nor any of the line-position methods, now in common practice for obtaining the ship's position. When approaching a port at night the ship was usually hove-to and got under way again at dawn. As will be seen, a considerable amount of delay could be occasioned in making a port.

The watch and watch method—four hours on duty followed by four hours off—was that employed in the windjammers. In the watch off duty, known as the 'watch below', everything such as getting meals, washing oneself and one's clothes and the accommodation had to be done, thus cutting down the small amount of sleeping time available. Then there was the all too frequent order 'all hands on deck' which often necessitated the whole of a long night spent in making sails fast. But in fine weather there was often the opportunity of sneaking a couple of hours' sleep at night in one's watch on deck. The 'all night in' obtained while the ship was in port was eagerly anticipated. To be able to sleep for eight hours, knowing that one's sleep would not be disturbed, was the most enjoyable experience in the windjammers.

With regard to junior officers in the last of the British windjammers the second mates rarely had certificates and were sometimes apprentices not out of their time as were the third mates. Whether apprentices or fo'c'sle seamen, the second mates, always known as 'acting' to avoid paying the full rate of wages, were usually signed on the ship's articles as bosuns (boatswains). Practical instances will be referred to in the following chapters.

The abbreviation 'fo'c'sle' for forecastle is always used by seamen whether they are referring to their living quarters or to the fo'c'sle head, the raised deck in the bows of the ship. As a seaman I will use it in this book. To prevent misunderstanding I have given the first mate his official designation 'first mate' although he was always called *the* mate in windjammers. In modern times he is known as the chief officer. The captain was, and is, generally called the 'Old Man', out of his hearing. In the windjammers the captain always addressed his mates as 'mister' rarely following with their surnames. I have omitted apostrophes in the word bosun purposely since it has become an established word in nautical phraseology.

As I mentioned earlier, the business side of Sir William Garthwaite's windjammer company is apt to be confusing with regard to the title of the firm, whether the ships were officially owned in Great Britain or Canada, at which port they were registered, which flag they flew and from which office they were managed. In this respect it is only possible to deal with individual ships. But this is established; the ships and barques were British built, were bought from British owners and the owner was an Englishman, in fact a Londoner, and the ships were run from a London office even though it might be termed an Agency. On the strength of this the author refers to the vessels and the firm that owned and managed them, as British. Now comes the story of the ships and barques and the men who served in them.

Chapter One

The early losses

The steel full-rigged ship *Queen Elizabeth*, 1,707 tons net, was the first vessel of Sir William Garthwaite's sailing ship fleet to be lost. She could have only been in his ownership list for about two months. He never even saw her. She was built in 1889 at Dumbarton by A McMillan & Sons and sold to Sir William in November, 1915 by the Queen Elizabeth Ship Company, managing owners Messrs Black, Moore and Company of 3 East India Avenue, London EC. Her master was Captain J H Quale and he sailed in her when she left Liverpool in ballast for Santos, Brazil, on the 2nd December, 1915. The last heard of her was when she signalled her name to a passing ship on the 21st December, when five miles to the south-west of Tuskar Rock (south-east point of Ireland). Wreckage from her was washed up in Cardigan Bay in January, 1916, and it seems probable that she was sunk by an enemy submarine late in December, 1915. No one was saved from her and she was posted missing on the 10th May, 1916.

The next two vessels of the Company to be sunk, both by German submarines, were the two three-masted steel barques *Invercauld* and the *Invermay* which were bought from the 'Inver' Line, George Milne and Company of Aberdeen, in 1916. The *Invercauld*, of 1,303 tons net, was purchased for £13,000. She had been built by A McMillan & Sons of Dumbarton in 1891 and was a particularly good sea-vessel, behaving well in heavy seas and being reasonably dry on deck. She sailed well when close hauled to the wind and on one memorable occasion beat all the famous German 'P' line sailing ships in a voyage home from a port on the West Coast of South America. She had no passenger accommodation but the quarters allocated to the master and officers, under the poop deck, were excellent by any sailing ship standard. In a big deck house between the foremast and the mainmast, was the fo'c'sle for the seamen, the 'half-deck' for the apprentices was just abaft it, and the galley was at the extreme after end.

Captain C J Mann commanded the *Invercauld* from 1911 to 1917. His wife sailed with him. He never attempted to make fast passages and was opposed to keeping sail set, when it was safer to have it made fast, in order to gain a few miles. He was popular with his officers and crews and his ships were always happy ones. They knew he would have the sails made fast in good time when bad weather threatened, and not leave it so late that high winds and heavy seas made it difficult and dangerous to haul the sails up and make them fast on the yards. But there was one criticism. At times he would order the royals and light fore and aft sails to be made fast before he turned in at night and would have them set when he came on deck early next morning. In this he was not alone; the author sailed under a master who did it regularly.

Captain Mann gave his apprentices lessons in seamanship and looked after their welfare on board. Life on board his ships was more comfortable than in most windjammers of his day, and his men showed their gratitude. No one took advantage of his kindness and consideration. His life was influenced by the terrible experience he had in 1894–1896 when first mate of the barque *Craigmullen*.

During a passage from Bangkok to Callao, the crew endured a hundred days' calm and ran short of fresh water in the Bashi Channel between the Philippines and Taiwan (Formosa). The passage took ten months to complete and the captain and all hands died at sea except the first and second mates and the sailmaker, the latter dying in hospital in Callao. The barque was picked up by a coasting steamer of the Pacific Steam Navigation Company and towed into Callao.

Captain Mann's first command in sail was the four-masted barquentine *Renfield* from 1908 to 1911. He then joined the *Invercauld* and remained in her until she was sunk. When the 1914–1918 world war began she was sailing across the South Pacific Ocean from Geelong in Australia to Valparaiso in Chile. She was delayed there until the ships of the German naval fleet, under Admiral von Spee, were sunk off the Falkland Islands, and then she sailed in ballast for Portland, Oregon, to load grain for Queenstown for orders. She sailed from Portland on the 19th February, 1915.

Before arriving at Queenstown she was given orders by a naval patrol ship to proceed direct to Dublin to discharge her cargo. Then she was towed across the Irish Sea to Birkenhead where Mr Colefield joined her as first mate and Mr Thomson, from Hull, as second mate. Apart from two cadets in the half deck and two British seamen in the fo'c'sle, all the other seamen were Scandinavians. It was at this time, in 1916, that the

Invercauld came under the ownership of William Garthwaite and she sailed in ballast to Gulfport in the Gulf of Mexico, where railway sleepers (timber) were loaded for Fleetwood, Lancashire.

On the morning of the 22nd February, 1917, when on the homeward passage, and lying becalmed 22 miles south-east of Mine Head, Waterford, the German submarine, U84, was sighted on the surface dead astern. One bell, 7.45 am, had just been struck and the watch below were having breakfast. The submarine made a wide circle round the *Invercauld* while the crew of the barque swung out the lifeboats ready for lowering. A warning shot was fired across the barque's bow and all hands left her in the two lifeboats. As soon as the boats were clear the barque was torpedoed on the starboard side. She heeled over. Captain Mann was called to the submarine and a German lieutenant and some of her ratings got into the boat, Captain Mann being ordered to take them to the barque. The Germans went on board and the lieutenant took the red ensign and the house flag and told his men to take what they wanted from the slop chest. This is the captain's shop from which he supplied the crew with their requirements during the voyage. In the meantime the lieutenant took the two chronometers and the ship's bell.

Captain Mann objected to this and protested to the German lieutenant who replied that as the barque was being sunk he could not see that it mattered. But to satisfy the Captain he gave a receipt for the things taken It read:

On the 22nd February, 1917, there was taken away from the English sailer *Invercauld.*

Two chronometers
One ship's bell
Underclothing
Several pieces of soap
Matches
One line

(signed) Keyzen
Sea Lieutenant

On arriving at the London office Captain Mann handed the receipt to his new owners.

Although the barque had listed over she had not sunk, no doubt because she was loaded with timber. Shells were then fired into the hull until she heeled right over and went to the bottom. Captain Mann was given the course and distance to the nearest land which he passed on to the first mate in the other lifeboat. Before they reached the shore they were picked up by a Glasgow-owned steamer and later transferred to the corvette, HMS *Buttercup* and landed at Queenstown. All hands were saved.

Captain Mann was later appointed master of the four-masted barque *Bellands*, ex *Forteviot* and in 1922 joined Sir William Garthwaite's *Garthwray* as master for her last voyage. He did not complete this voyage.

The *Invermay*, a three-masted barque of 1,337 tons, was built in 1895 by Russell & Company of Port Glasgow for George Milne's 'Inver' Line of Aberdeen. The author's research discovered that she was sold to R W G Sutherland of Cardiff for £15,000 in 1916 and The Marine Navigation Company (William Garthwaite) became her owners in the same year. Commander F A C Bishop, making his first voyage to sea, joined her at Newport, Mon, in the Bristol Channel when she was loaded with coals. She sailed for Barry Roads on the 9th November, 1916. There the barque lay at anchor for a week waiting Admiralty sailing orders, and then left for Buenos Aires arriving on the 13th January, 1917.

Captain Henry H Lawrence of County Antrim, Northern Ireland, was her master and he had served in the barque when she was owned by George Milne. He was then 61 years of age. He had been in command of the famous *Peter Iredale* and was described as 'a hard case of the old school of sailing ship masters'. The first mate was a 69-year-old Londoner, then living in Liverpool, named Robert Chamberlain, who had previously been master of the *Dimsdale*. In spite of his age he was very hardy and carried out his duties as well as many first mates who were much younger. The second mate, who was signed on the ship's articles as bosun—presumably because he did not then hold a second mate's certificate—was a competent young officer, later Captain H M Brown, MBE.

Although the port of registry of the *Invermay* was given as Montreal, her owners and their address, was recorded in her official documents as The Marine Navigation Company Limited, of 92 Gracechurch Street, London EC. In Lloyd's Register of Shipping, the main office of the firm was given as 7, Rue Meyerbeer, Paris.

After the coals were discharged at Buenos Aires a full cargo of grain was loaded for Londonderry and the *Invermay* sailed on the 14th February, 1917.

When the barque was about 40 miles north-west of Eagle Island off the west coast of Ireland, in latitude 54° 50′ north, longitude 11° west at 6.30 am on the 25th April, 1917, the second mate, who was lying in his bunk, was awoken by the stamping of feet on the poop over his head and the shouting of Captain Lawrence to 'back the main yards'. He dashed out on deck to the lee main braces and slacked away while the watch hauled on the weather braces and hauled the yards round on the other tack. When he had time to look round he saw a big submarine, well away from the barque on the port side. The *Invermay* had been sailing at about four knots braced sharp up on the starboard tack. The submarine opened fire and the first shot went through the fore lower topsail, the second hitting the fore royal yard. Captain Lawrence ordered the lifeboats to be swung out and lowered, and the steward and cabin boy put food into them, the water casks already being filled.

By this time the submarine had submerged, and, after going round the barque with her periscope showing above the surface of the sea, she surfaced again near the barque's bow and fired three shots purposely aimed high. By this time the crew had left the barque in the two lifeboats. The submarine put one of her boats into the sea and the crew pulled over to the *Invermay*. They were on board about twenty minutes during which time they looted the barque and placed time bombs in her stern. Soon after they left there was a terrific explosion and her stern blew off. She settled down aft and her bow lifted up into the air until her masts lay horizontally on the surface of the sea. She slid under the water with her jib boom sticking vertically into the air. The last thing her crew saw of her from the boats was the shark's tail on the end of the jib boom.

Everything was done promptly on board when the barque was

abandoned, all orders being carried out when they were given with no sign of panic. Commander Bishop remembers being ordered to haul in the line of the patent log and coil it up neatly on the poop. To him this seemed unnecessary, especially as the rest of the crew were getting into the lifeboats to abandon ship.

The crew hoisted the sails of their boats and set a course to the eastward with the help of a light to moderate westerly wind. Part of the time they rowed and twenty-four hours passed before they reached the coast. They landed at Ballyglass Coastguard station at 6 am on the 26th April, and were taken by jaunting cars to a small town and then on to the nearest railway station in motor lorries. They went by train to Dublin and sailed to Liverpool where they arrived on Saturday night without a penny between them. There was only room for the second mate in the Sailors' Home but he got the crew into the Cunard Home for the week-end and they paid off on Monday. Captain Lawrence took the three apprentices to London and sent them off to their homes after reporting to the owners' office at 92/94 Gracechurch Street, London.

Less than three weeks after the *Invermay* was sunk the *Carnmoney* was sent to the bottom by a submarine. She was an iron three-masted barque of 1,255 tons net, built by Workman, Clark & Company of Belfast in 1884 for W Porter & Sons of Belfast and sold to John Stewart & Company in 1898. Captain G Dennison had been her master since 1912 and went over to the new owners with the barque. Her first mate on this voyage was Mr F O Bindberg from Finland.

On her first voyage for William Garthwaite she sailed on the 27th November, 1915 for Bahia Blanca where she arrived on the 23rd February, 1916. There she loaded a full cargo of wheat, and sailed for St Nazaire, France, on the 23rd March, 1916. The Log Book for this voyage gave the owner as William Garthwaite, 75 Mark Lane, London EC. On the next voyage this address was pasted over with: 92 Gracechurch Street, London EC.

On the passage home from Bahia Blanca the *Carnmoney* drowned her second and third mates. This is the entry in the Official Log:

6th April, 1916. Latitude 35° 30′ south, longitude 36° 20′ west. Taking in the reefed foresail to a heavy south-east increasing gale with high sea the 2nd mate, W B Williams and the third mate P Olsen, observing the inner jib adrift, went out [on the jib boom] to make it fast and later, the vessel dipping to a cross-sea, they fell overboard and were drowned. On my hearing the [warning] cry from aloft I saw the 3rd mate in the water to windward. I immediately ran and threw overboard the [spanker] boom sheet and log line, ordering the helm down at the same time. The vessel was under two lower topsails and goose-winged reefed foresail and mizzen and fore topmast stay sails, driving to a heavy beam increasing gale and sea, she putting the lee rail under and shipping heavy lee water, so that it was impossible to launch the lifeboat without having it smashed to pieces, and all hands declare that even if the lifeboat could have been launched it could not have been handled in such a sea and gale but would have been driven away and lost. The 2nd mate was observed to sink immediately after falling as if hurt and unconscious and the 3rd mate was quickly lost from sight. Both men were in sea boots and oilskins.

George Dennison, Master.

To have attempted to launch the boat would have meant having it smashed to atoms, but even if the boat could have been launched no crew could have pulled to windward into such a sea and gale. Immediately after falling the second mate was observed to be laying motionless with head down as if hurt and unconscious.

Signed by F O Bindberg, Mate,
and a number of the crew.

The second mate Mr W B Williams was 24 years of age and came from Caernarvon, Wales. The third mate, Mr P Olsen, was 26, and came from Norway. I have met this type of man on board sailing ships. They are heroes, of course, but whether they realise the danger which they are exposed to, or expose themselves to, or whether it has become second nature to them so that they are not as careful as they should be, is hard to say and certainly no criticism can be offered.

From St Nazaire the *Carnmoney* sailed on the 27th July, 1916, in ballast, for Norfolk, Virginia, on the east coast of the United States of America, arriving on the 11th September. She left loaded for Montevideo on the 7th October and arrived there on the 20th December, 1916. After discharging her cargo there she proceeded to Buenos Aires to load maize for the United Kingdom and left on the 8th February, 1917.

Captain Dennison had been relieved at Norfolk on the 28th September, 1916, by Captain J H Shippen. Mrs Shippen accompanied him and signed on the ship's articles as stewardess. The passage home from Buenos Aires was the last the *Carnmoney* made for at 9.30 am on the 14th May, 1917, in latitude 50° 20′ north and longitude 13° 10′ west, she was sunk by gunfire and bombs placed in the hold by the crew of a German submarine. All hands got safely away in the two lifeboats. After three days in the boats, when Gull Rock was bearing north-east, ten miles distant, they were picked up by the SS *Hatumed* and landed in Glasgow. All hands were saved.

Chapter Two

The *Garthforce*

The *Garthforce* was launched as the *Iquique* in 1892 from the yard of W Hamilton & Company of Port Glasgow. She was a steel, three-masted full-rigged ship of 1,859 tons net. When she was sold to the Celtic Line, W Hugh-Jones and Company of 18 Water Street, Liverpool, her name was changed to *Celtic Glen*. In 1917 she was owned by Glen, Ford and Company Limited of Birmingham and loaded coals at Barry Dock, leaving for Buenos Aires on the 29th August. On this voyage Captain John Henry of Dumfries was her master and he remained in command of her for the rest of her sea-going days. He was considered one of the most efficient sailing ship captains of his day. Mr John F Collins was her first mate and Mr A C Zrinyi her second mate. Both were first rate officers.

The name *Celtic Glen* was changed to *Riverford* after the Birmingham Company bought her and she retained the name when William Garthwaite took her over which was probably towards the end of 1917. She was still the *Riverford* when she arrived at New York on the 23rd August, 1918. It is probable that her name was changed to *Garthforce* before she left; especially as her voyage finished there and new Articles were signed. The Official Log kept at that time had on its cover: *Riverford*, ex *Celtic Glen*, now *Garthforce*. Her port of registry remained as Liverpool. Lloyd's Register of Shipping for 1917–18 gave the name of William Garthwaite's firm as 'The Marine Navigation Company of 92/94 Gracechurch Street, London EC, but after the edition was published a correction was made by pasting a new title over the original. This was: 'The Marine Navigation Company of Canada, Limited.'

Captain R E Clare, who was serving at the time of writing as a Trinity House Channel Pilot, based on Dover, Kent, and a member of 'The International Association of Master Mariners—Cape Horners', joined the *Celtic Glen* as an apprentice at the end of 1915 and left her when she was named *Garthforce* at the end of 1920. On her first voyage for The Marine Navigation Company, the *Riverford*, after discharging her coals in Buenos Aires, left in ballast for Geelong (Melbourne) Australia, arriving there on the 14th March, 1918. There she loaded wheat in bags for New York and sailed on the 14th April. It was while on this passage that, in the North Atlantic to the eastward of the West Indies, the ship experienced a hurricane force gale which threw her right over on to her beam ends.

In the first dog watch (4 pm to 6 pm) the weather was fine and the sea calm; the yards were braced sharp up on the port tack and all seemed set for a get-together sing-song in the half deck in the second dog-watch (6 pm to 8 pm) when the officer of the watch blew two whistles for his watch to come on deck and reduce sail. The ship was then snugged down to the topsails and foresails, and, instead of a sing-song, all hands were aloft in the second dog-watch making sail fast. The lads in the half deck were scathingly critical about 'the old women aft' (the captain and mates) who had started to take in sail before there was any sign of an increase in wind. Even so, when they got out on deck they saw that the sky to the south-east was dark and rugged with sharply-edged clouds of blue-black appearance; and they could not help noticing that the air was damp and heavy, and, although the sky overhead was blue, the sunset was a yellowish-green. In the first night watch (8 pm to midnight) the fore and mizzen upper topsails were furled and made fast.

At three o'clock next morning it was 'all hands on deck'. The ship had been suddenly hove-down on to her side by a terrific squall. The lee side of the ship was under water up to the hatch coamings. It was as dangerous a position for a ship as could be. All hands tried to get the main upper topsail off the ship but they could not get the yard lowered down the mast, for the angle of heel of the ship and the weight of the wind in the sail was causing it to jam.

'All right!' said Mr Collins the first mate, to young Clare and a fellow apprentice standing near. 'Up aloft and cut the sheets.' It was a hazardous job but they climbed aloft to the main top and were able to cut the sheets there. The weight of wind in the sail was released as it banged in the hurricane force wind, enabling the sail to be hauled up to the yard which could then be lowered down the mast.

Then came the biggest and hardest job of all—taking the big foresail in and making it fast. All hands, except the man at the wheel, were needed for this job—even the cook if he was young and able enough to give a few pounds pull on a rope. The weather was as bad as it could be;

wind and sea were both dangerous; it was dark and the ship was still heeled over dangerously. Two able seamen were sent up on the forecastle head to slack away the tack—the rope holding down the weather corner of the sail—while the rest of the hands pulled on the clew garnets to haul the sail up to the yard-arm.

'Slack away the tack!' yelled Mr Collins, who was supervising the operation. There was no answer and nothing happened. 'Slack away that tack! What the hell's wrong up there!' Mr Collins shouted even louder. Still no answer so he went up the fo'c'sle head ladder from the fore deck to see what was wrong. The two men were not there. They were never found. They must have been blown over the side—there were only rails at the side there instead of solid bulwarks—or have been washed overboard. No one saw them go and not a sound or a cry for help was heard. It was not absolutely sure at that time that they had gone overboard. But with the ship in the dangerous position she was, and the big seas running, it would have been impossible to get a lifeboat away. So Mr Collins, who was 55 years of age, remained in the position of danger and slacked away the tack single-handed while the hands pulled on the clew-lines, leechlines and buntlines, to haul the sail as snug as possible up to the yard. The second mate had taken charge on the fore deck. They were two fine officers; always in the lead where danger was apparent.

Now came the worst job—making the sails fast to the yards which were now more vertical than horizontal. A foothold could not be obtained on the foot ropes under the yards on which the hands had to try to stand; feet slid down the wire until they came to a nearly horizontal stirrup which was normally vertical. The foresail was the worst job. It was a big sail of heavy No 1 canvas some 80 feet long by 40 feet deep; wet and almost as hard as metal, blown into huge sections or bellies by the wind and held between the buntlines.

The ship returned more to the upright after the topsail and foresail were taken off her; but even so, the men working on the lee fore yard arm were occasionally dipped into the sea. The air was saturated with a fine mist which made the seamen's eyes water copiously and added to the difficulties and terrors of that awful night.

Captain Clare quoted from a memory which was still vivid:

> The squall and the rain had passed; the wind was hurricane force from the north-west with a heavy sea and a big south-easterly swell. I glanced aft from the fore yard, and, as the moon showed through the racing clouds, caught a fitful glimpse of the 'Old Man' [captain] on the poop and the man at the wheel. The 'Old Man' was still in his pyjamas.

It took most of two hours to get the foresail snugged up on that yard and secured with the gaskets; and all but three were up there—not counting the two men lost overboard. The two mates were there and only the captain, the man at the wheel and the cook, who was no doubt trying to prepare hot coffee in a galley that had been almost swept bare by the crashing seas, were down on deck.

When the ship arrived in New York on the 23rd August, 1918, she still had a list to starboard even though some of the cargo had been shifted up to the port or high side. She was moored in the Eyrie Basin close to the *Wray Castle*, later to be renamed the *Garthwray*, and the *Juteopolis* to be renamed the *Garthpool*. This was in the summer of 1918 when the Spanish Influenza epidemic was spreading fast in New York.

Most of the apprentices in these three ships caught it and some died. Captain Clare remembered that there were three other apprentices with him from the *Garthforce* and four from the *Wray Castle* in a ward in the Flatbush Avenue Cottage Hospital. There they were treated very kindly and to them it was a rest cure. They had a very likeable Irish nurse, a redhead, who was a good sport. But she used to get 'hopping mad' when they threw orange peel at a big portrait in colours of the American sailor, Admiral Sims.

The *Garthforce* sailed from New York on the 14th October, 1918, with a cargo for Melbourne. Her owners were then recorded as 'The Marine Navigation Company, Montreal' although her port of registry was still Liverpool. She arrived at Melbourne on the 25th January, 1919, and since her owners were unable to get a cargo to load there, they sent her north to Newcastle to load coals for Iquique. On this passage the usual bad weather was experienced and she arrived at the Chilean port on the 23rd June. There, after discharging her coals with the hand dolly winch, she loaded nitrate for a 'round the Horn' passage to Cape Town, arriving there on the 24th October, 1919. This was the end of the voyage and the Ships Articles were terminated and the officers and crew were paid off.

On the next voyage the *Garthforce* left Cape Town in ballast on the 26th November, 1919, for Newcastle, Australia, in a fresh west-north-westerly wind. It increased to a moderate gale and drove the ship across the South Indian Ocean to the Bass Strait where one of Australia's notorious 'Southerly Busters' was experienced. This meant sail being reduced to the fore and main lower topsails. Up till then she had carried the six topsails with a reefed mainsail and reefed topgallant sails.

She arrived on the 27th January, 1920, and it was early in March, just before the *Garthforce* left Newcastle for Iquique with a cargo of coals, that Captain Henry went to the half deck at breakfast time and called for young Clare who was enjoying a plate of burgoo (oatmeal made with water) and molasses. 'Take your traps into the second Mate's room!' he ordered. Thus was his promotion announced a few days before his nineteenth birthday. He was allowed to finish his burgoo.

This time it was a summer passage across the South Pacific in the roaring forties and good time was made, the *Garthforce* arriving at Valparaiso on the 25th April. Her coals unloaded, she sailed up the Chilean coast to Taltal to load nitrate for Falmouth for orders and left on the 9th June, 1920. This gave her a winter rounding of Cape Horn but she made good time, arriving on the 16th November after a passage of 109 days. At Falmouth her orders came through for her discharging port. It was Liverpool and she arrived three on the 26th November, 1920, after being away from home for three years and three months.

On the next voyage of the *Garthforce* young Carter, now Captain Charles E Carter of Mosman, New South Wales, Australia, joined her to start his apprenticeship. He signed his Indentures on the 16th December, 1920, but did not join the ship in Birkenhead until March 1921. It was not until the 10th November that she sailed from the Powder Grounds in the River Mersey with a cargo of rock salt and gunpowder for Sydney, Australia.

The seven apprentices were all first voyagers, and as they were to experience more than their fair share of disaster at sea, it may be of interest to mention their names. They were Lionel Adams of Brighton, Charles E B Carter of East Ham, London, Leslie M Rolfe of Maidstone, Kent, Thomas G Ward of London, Vincent W Martin of London, Francis S J Butcher of Hull, and George A Kent of Liverpool. Lionel Adams is now Chairman of the Australian Canned Fruits Board and Captain C E Carter, who has made Australia his home since his sailing ship days, became Marine Superintendent, and later, Shipping Department Manager of the Colonial Sugar Refining Company. With Lionel Adams, he has founded The Australian Sail Training Association and is hoping, with public support, to have a barquentine of 350 tons built for sea training. Going aloft to make sail fast on the foremast will be an invaluable addition to a three months training course at sea.

The seven apprentices joined the ship some months before she sailed and consequently gained experience on deck and aloft before sailing. When the tug left the ship on the outward passage they loosed the top-sails, and two days later, when out in the North Atlantic, they were aloft on the fore yard in a strong gale helping to make the foresail fast.

Captain John Henry was still master of the *Garthforce*, Mr D Cruickshank, who held a master's certificate and had been master in sail, was first mate and Mr W Loades second mate. There was an exceptionally good crew in the fo'c'sle, all Britishers. There was a good deal of unemployment among seamen at this time which enabled Captain Henry to choose his crew. That voyage the *Garthforce* carried 14 able seamen and two ordinary seamen besides the bosun, sailmaker, carpenter, steward, cook, the apprentices and the two mates. This is a big crew at that time for a sailing ship of the tonnage of the *Garthforce*.

She sailed to the southward on the usual sailing ship track, sighting Tristan da Cunha in 37° south and then, as was Captain Henry's usual practice, setting course to the south and east to run the easting down nearer

50° south than 40° south. On the 27th January, 1922, the ship passed two miles to the southward of Prince Edward Island, some thousand miles south-east of the Cape of Good Hope. She was sailing at ten knots at the time, but the wind was increasing from the north-west and in the second dog-watch the royals were hauled up and young Adams and a fellow apprentice were sent aloft to make the main royal fast on the yard. From their high advantage point they could see Marion Island, latitude 46° 52′ south, longitude 38° east. It is a larger island than Prince Edward and is about 3,890 feet high, thirteen miles long and eight miles wide. Since 1948 the Union of South Africa have claimed it and established a Meteorological Station there. It was also reported to have a depot for shipwrecked mariners at the time the *Garthforce* passed it, but neither of the lads could see any sign of it.

The wind increased and in the first night watch (8 pm to midnight) the three topgallant sails and the mainsail were made fast. At midnight, when the second mate's watch came on deck, the ship was running under the six topsails, the foresail, the three topmast staysails and the inner jib. Shortly before two o'clock in that early morning watch, the second mate, an excellent seaman and officer, considered it prudent to take in and make fast the mizzen and main topmast staysails. The mizzen was hauled down first and young Carter and Kent were told off to make it fast while the remainder of the watch went forward to haul down the main topmast staysail.

The second mate was waiting at the main rigging to cast off the halliards from the belaying pin, and Carter and Kent were balancing themselves on the top of the flywheels of the pumps at the main fife-rails, making the mizzen topmast staysail fast, when the man on the look-out on the fo'c'sle head shouted: 'Ice ahead!' It was raining and visibility was low. Almost immediately the two apprentices heard a jarring, tearing noise and the ship brought up dead, throwing them off the flywheels down on to the deck. Young Carter fell on to his back and looking forward saw the whole of the foremast, about 180 feet in height, silhouetted against an enormous iceberg. The watch ran aft shouting as they went while the watch below tumbled out of their bunks and followed their shipmates.

Then Captain Henry appeared on the poop, fully clothed, and restored order amongst his crew.

Perhaps the best description of the collision was contributed to *The Australian Walkabout Magazine* by Lionel Adams:

'The look-out on the forecastle head, peering through the torrential rain, shouted 'Ice!' and in an instant came a tremendous smashing noise as the thousands of tons of ship and cargo crashed at over twelve miles an hour into millions of tons of iceberg. The shriek of tearing steel and the shuddering of every part of the ship's fabric as it seemed to crumple under the stress, was followed by a huge rolling sea that burst right over the groaning vessel and then hurled her again at the iceberg. As the ship lay with great seas pounding aboard, a faint green blink from the iceberg seemed to dimly illuminate her. There was no other light, for the lamps in the sleeping quarters had been put out, while cupboard drawers had been slung open, bunks were wrenched apart, and there was water and chaos everywhere.

To add to the terror the ship gave two terrific bumps against the iceberg and tons of ice fell on board. The main deck from the mizzen hatch to the fo'c'sle head was a huge river of water running towards the sinking bow, and it was through and against this that men were hauling themselves along by the lifelines to what appeared to be the safety of the poop aft. With this fighting crowd was the cook, a small frail figure of a man, being hauled along by his collar by a huge blaspheming Liverpool Irishman.

The more sober report of the 'Official Log' gives a terse description. As in all entries in the 'Official Log' there is just enough information to cover the incident; short and written with economy:

Garthforce from Liverpool towards Sydney, Australia, 28.1.22 at 2 am, Latitude 46° 48′ south, Longitude 39° 46′ east. Vessel sailing under topsails, foresail and three lower staysails and inner jib, wind strong from northward, squally with rain, steering full and bye on the port tack. At about 2 am iceberg seen close on weather bow. Helm was at once put hard up, but before ship's head had time to fall off, struck iceberg and carrying away [jib] boom and all head gear ship continued pounding at berg until the main yards having been thrown aback, the vessel then backed off clear of berg; forward, fore peak full of water, no water in well. Swung out and provisioned port and starboard lifeboats. At 6 am all yards, masts and rigging above the fore lower mast head came down on deck. At 7 am all hands commenced to clear away the wreckage; ship not under command, drifting with wind and sea. No accident to any of the crew; at most found forepeak full of water and 4½ inches of water in the well. Got main pumps rigged for emergency.

Signed by master, 1st mate, 2nd mate, carpenter and two able seamen.

That was the official report. There is nothing to find fault with there, unless it could be said that the ship was carrying too much sail and doing too much speed, in weather that included heavy, blinding rain squalls. But the crew were taking in sail when the iceberg was struck and no ice had been reported before the accident. As far as the author knows there was no criticism of Captain Henry's handling of the ship. As had already been said it was his practice to sail his ship across the South Indian Ocean in latitudes approaching the fifties. There are less miles in the degrees of longitude there than further north, and, no doubt, his experience had taught him that quicker passages could be made by sailing across more to the southward. The masters under whom I served believed the reverse and the barques I sailed in always ran their easting down between 38° and 42° south. On one passage I remember meeting head winds, but once we made a record passage of 22 days in the *Lorton* from Durban to Adelaide. Naturally there was always a greater risk of meeting icebergs further south, and usually, the wind was stronger than was wanted for good speed. Of course there was always the element of luck in making good (short) or long passages. One might say that this also applies to hitting icebergs in blinding rain squalls.

On board the *Garthforce*, orders were given to swing out the lifeboats,

2

ready for abandoning ship, which was a dangerous job. They were on the skids on each side of the bridge, some eight feet above the main deck and twenty feet forward of the poop. While the crew were engaged in hoisting the port lifeboat off the skids, to swing her outboard in the davits, a tremendous sea came up from the quarter and carried the boat away over the side. She was lost and it was lucky that none of the crew were washed overboard as well. It was at this time that the ship was flung clear of the iceberg.

Water was reported to be making fast in the well of the ship at the main hold. Captain Henry did not believe this possible and he sent young Adams down the main ventilator to make certain. He had to go down an iron ladder in a small vertical shaft. It must have been frightening, especially as the small hatch on the main deck level had to be put on and fastened down to prevent the seas flooding down the shaft. It was the only way out for Adams, and, after he had been right down to the bottom of the ship, found no water, and climbed up to the deck only to find that he could get no response to his banging on the underneath of the hatch and shouting at the top of his voice, he began to wonder if he would ever get out alive.

It was found that the fore peak was full of water but the forward watertight bulkhead, between the fore peak and No 1 hold, was holding the weight of water and not leaking. Although the ship was badly down by the head she did not seem in any immediate danger. At daylight the iceberg was still in sight and it was estimated to be about 1½ miles in length, 600 feet in height and almost rectangular in shape.

The bowsprit of the *Garthforce* had been turned round about 75° to port and its heel, torn away from its stop under the fore end of the fo'c'sle head, was resting hard against the frames of the ship on the starboard side. The ship's side plating was ripped wide open. Fortunately the crew were not accommodated under the fo'c'sle head or none would have survived, but a loud miowing was heard coming from there. It appeared that 'Ginger', the ship's cat, had been sleeping on a shelf in the paint locker when the collision caused it to collapse and dropped him into a barrel of tar from which he managed to lift his head but not the rest of his body. He was rescued promptly, wiped down with kerosine (paraffin) oil, and was none the worse for his adventure.

The foremast was swaying dangerously and its loose gear was swinging from side to side with the rolling of the ship. Then with a shuddering that shook the whole ship, and a slow backward movement, the whole jumbled mass aloft came crashing down dragging the main topgallant mast forward and down with it. There were cross patterns of wire and tangled rope aloft and on the fore deck; the fore upper topsail yard fell overboard and took up a position as a battering ram against the ship's side. There was a danger of her being holed under water, and immediate action, however dangerous, was imperative. The yard was being held from aloft by a wire backstay and from the deck by its gear. A line was passed round the backstay to hold the yard firmly against the side of the ship while the gear, holding it from sinking, was cut away with cold chisels and axes. The decks were continually swept by heavy seas and there was the ever-present danger of the cut wires whipping round and injuring or sweeping one of the crew overboard. When finally the backstay was cut, the yard fell to the bottom of the sea.

There was a current belief in sailing ships that 'to cut away the masts', to relieve dangerous heeling over of the ship, or to clear wreckage in a partially dismasted ship, it was only necessary to hit the metal box screws, which were just above the main deck and by which the shrouds or backstays were fitted to the chain plates, with a heavy topmaul to break it and then the shroud or backstay would immediately be cast adrift. This proved to be a fallacy. Hacksaws had to be used to saw through the heavy wires which was a long and tiring job.

An unusual bit of luck was experienced when the yards came down from aloft, the royal yard fell on to the deck just forward of the boat on the deck house and the topgallant yard on the deck just abaft it, just missing the boat. It will be remembered that the port lifeboat on the after skids had been washed overboard.

The upper topsails on the main and mizzen masts had been made fast as soon as possible, but with no headsails the ship was barely under control. Captain Henry decided to steer to the northward to cross the tracks of steamships bound for Australia, but little progress was made.

Two days later, after the wreckage had been cleared and a survey of the holds revealed no damage to the side plating of the ship, another iceberg was sighted. Captain Henry took bearings of it anxiously and found it remained on collision point; the ship was being carried towards it. There was only one thing to do, and that was to get more speed on the ship by setting the main and mizzen upper topsails. It was particularly risky on the mainmast where the topgallant mast had gone, especially as it was blowing half a gale with a fairly high sea. But those sails were loosed and set in record time and it was with great relief that captain and crew saw their ship increase speed, pass across the front of the iceberg and finally leave it astern.

It was found necessary to lighten the ship forward by dumping part of the cargo of rock salt overboard from the fore hatch. There were some cargo baskets in the hold and tubs were made from salt meat barrels. A temporary fore-and-aft stay was rigged over the fore hold and a single block was hung on it over the centre of the fore hatchway. A single rope was rove through it, one end with a hook on it going down into the hold to hook on the basket or tub, and the other end down through another block on the fore deck and lead horizontally along the deck for the crew to pull on. When the basket or tub was hoisted high enough to swing over to the bulwarks the contents were tipped over the side into the sea. This was easy enough in the still waters of a dock, but with the fore deck low down in the water and the ship taking heavy seas over, it was not only difficult to accomplish but also extremely dangerous. Sea shanties helped here, and although no one had enough breath to sing them, as they stamped and walked that rope along the deck to raise the tubs and baskets out of the hold, young Clarence Chugg, a very young ordinary seaman, played his flute to the tunes and the crew took their time from his playing.

Clarence was the son of Captain Chugg of Melbourne, Australia and it was the youth's intention to follow the sea as his profession but he failed the eyesight test and took up music as his career. He became an excellent flautist and pianist. He was, and probably is now, the leading flautist in the Australian Broadcasting Commission's Orchestra and ran his own dance band. But I dare to say that never were his musical efforts so much appreciated as during the time when he helped his shipmates haul that rock salt out of the fore hold of the *Garthforce.* It was not easy filling the tubs and baskets in the hold for it was impossible for the crew down there to keep their hands clear of the salt and painful sea-cuts resulted, which refused to heal up. Altogether 41 tons of rock salt and 6 tons of ship's stores were dumped overboard.

The dangerous gunpowder in the square at the top of the main hatch was also jettisoned. Captain Henry had been worried about that from the time that the yards and gear came hurtling down from aloft. It was not the type of cargo that one could be happy about in a damaged ship. An entry in the Official Log reads:

> At 9 am on the 6th February, 1922, in latitude 40° 45′ south, longitude 45° 19′ east, 3,199 cases of gunpowder, each weighing 56 lbs were jettisoned from the main hold to get the ship under command.

One incident that occurred before the collision throws some light on one of the sailor's superstitions. Eight days before the *Garthforce* hit the iceberg the first mate caught an albatross by the usual method of towing an open triangle of narrow brass strips, with salt pork fat tied on each strip, from the stern of the ship. The albatross trying to peck at the erratically moving bait on the surface of the sea with its huge, sharply curved-at-the-bottom beak, would get its beak through the inside of the triangle, then the line would be tightened on board and the albatross would be unable to release its beak. It would then be hauled on board and landed on deck where it would be seasick. The older sailors would always ask for it to be released at once because of their superstition that each albatross holds the soul of a departed seaman. The reason for this belief was that albatross would accompany sailing ships for thousands of miles in the roaring forties (latitude 40° to 50° south). It was sometimes said that they did so for the scraps of food that were thrown overboard from the galley. These albatross sometimes have a span of fourteen feet from tip to tip of wing. They are usually seen only in the southern hemisphere and not often north of latitude 30° south.

When the first mate caught the albatross Captain Henry asked for it to be released. He pointed out the bad luck that would follow the ship if it was not returned to the sea unharmed. Unfortunately it was killed.

A jury foresail was rigged and set and a course was made towards the coast of South Africa. There was one continuous worry. Would the watertight forward bulkhead hold against the full weight of the sea to which it was being directly subjected by the ship making headway? If the bulkhead carried away, nothing could save the ship and there would be only the boats for the crew. It would be a dangerous experience in the heavy seas of those latitudes.

At 4 pm on the 12th February, 1922, in latitude 35° 36′ south, longitude 48° 21′ east, fifteen days after the ship had struck the iceberg, a steamer was sighted on the starboard bow. She was the Swedish-owned *Unden* of Goteborg. She altered course and rounded up alongside the *Garthforce*. Captain Henry shouted across a request that his damaged ship be towed into port. The master of the steamer communicated by wireless with his owners and it was decided that the *Garthforce* be towed to Durban. No agreement was made.

There was a big swell running and attempts were made to float a line from the steamer to the sailing ship without success, so the *Unden* steamed slowly along the starboard side of the *Garthforce* and a heaving line was thrown on to the latter's fo'c'sle head. Then a stouter rope was passed across and finally a heavy wire was pulled aboard the sailing ship and shackled on to the end of her anchor cable. The latter was to be paid out to the 30 fathom shackle and then made fast. It ran out of the hawse pipe too quickly and when the carpenter tried to check its speed after 15 fathoms had run out, it brought up suddenly and the towing wire broke. The cable was hove in on the *Garthforce* and the wire on the *Unden* and the whole process had to be started again with a new wire. This time the cable was allowed to run out to 75 fathoms before it was checked and stopped. This gave the advantage of a long downward loop of the combined wire and chain cable which acted as a spring, smoothing and easing what would have been a sudden jerk capable of breaking the wire.

The chain cable was taken off the sailing ship's windlass, lead aft and made additionally secure round the mooring bitts and the foot of the foremast. Tackles were also made fast to the cable and tightened up to take some of the weight off the towing wire and cables.

On board the *Unden*, towing springs were rigged from her windlass, along both sides of her deck to her mooring bitts on the poop aft where they were made fast and continued over the stern in the form of a bridle and shackled to the towing wire.

On the seventh day of the tow the ships had arrived about 20 miles off the African coast and here the Agulhas Current flowing against the freshening south-east wind set up a nasty sea and the two ships rolled and pitched heavily. There was a risk of the tow rope parting. Inky black clouds began to bank up to windward with the danger of the onset of a black south-easter so much dreaded on that coast. The master of the *Unden* signalled to the *Garthforce*: 'Will have to turn to windward! Will put out oil on the sea and stand by with our lifeboats!'

The bad weather did not materialize and the ships soon got back on their course. An entry made in the Official Log of the *Garthforce* read:

> 19.2.22, 11.45 pm. This is to certify that the SS *Unden* towed the ship *Garthforce* into Port Natal [Durban] Bay on this date, after having the vessel in tow from Friday 12.2.22.

A Durban tug put the ship alongside the quay on the next morning and her cargo was discharged. Mr Lionel Adams wrote of the SS *Unden*:

> None of us ever saw or knew the group of people to whom we in the *Garthforce* owed our lives, except for one vague, large, white-sweatered figure on the bridge when the tow line was first passed, certain little midget figures that struggled daily with the grinding wires, and the imagined people who sent laconic messages regarding positions, speed and weather.

The *Garthforce* was on charter to Gracie Beasley & Company Limited, 14 Water Street, Liverpool. She was handed over to the underwriters as a total loss and sold for £500 to be used as a coal hulk. In November 1926 she was sold for breaking up and was cut down almost to her water line, and, while being towed to Simonstown, broke adrift from the tug and sank in deep water. Another story was that she was towed out to sea and sank on the 1st July, 1927. The author is of the opinion that the first record is correct.

She had gone through the collision and dismasting without any accident to the crew, but while lying safely alongside the wharf at Durban, at 10 am on the 9th March, 1922, Vincent Holden, sailor age 34, whose home was at St John's, Newfoundland, was killed. He was assisting in sending the main topgallant mast down on deck, and fell from the crosstrees to the deck, to be killed instantly.

Chapter Three

The *Garthsnaid*

The *Garthsnaid* was a three-masted barque of 1,312 tons net built in 1892 by A McMillan & Son, Limited, of Dumbarton as the *Inversnaid*. She was bought at the end of 1916 by William Garthwaite of The Marine Navigation Company, then of 94 Gracechurch Street, London EC, for £15,000 and sailed from Port Talbot, South Wales, on the 5th January, 1917, loaded with coals for Rio de Janeiro, Brazil. Captain Syviet was her master. He was a bearded Channel Islander always friendly disposed to his crews. Her first mate on this voyage was Mr John Taggart of Cumberland, aged 69, who signed on at £18 a month; and Mr A Bicknell, an Australian from Melbourne, aged 26, was in the barque's Crew Agreement as bosun and acting second mate at £11.10s a month.

Still named *Inversnaid* she arrived at Rio de Janeiro on the 25th February, 1917, and, after discharging her cargo, sailed north to Santos in ballast to load for Queenstown, southern Ireland, for orders, arriving there on the 17th July. It was here that Commander F A C Bishop, RNR, of Dorset, joined her as an apprentice and sailed in her on the 30th July for her discharging port, Le Havre, in northern France, where she arrived on the 6th August, 1917. This completed her first voyage under the ownership of William Garthwaite.

The *Inversnaid* sailed for Port Talbot on the 15th September, to load coals again for Rio de Janeiro, but she did not get away from the Welsh port until the 3rd December. Then she was towed to Milford Haven where she waited a week to complete her crew. Apart from the fact that there were few qualified sailing ship seamen available in English ports at this time, a sailing ship was often a squatting target for a submarine and many were being sunk. Young apprentices were in increasing demand to man and sail them, and there was no shortage of applications from them.

In Lloyd's Register of Shipping of 1917–18, the *Inversnaid* was overprinted as being owned by 'The Marine Navigation Company of Canada, Limited, Montreal, British'; but in the Official Board of Trade Crew Agreement, dated 28th July, 1917, she was still registered at Aberdeen and her owner's title and address was given as: 'The Marine Navigation Company Limited, 92/94 Gracechurch Street, London EC.'

On this voyage her crew and captain numbered twenty-three. There were eight able seamen, two ordinary seamen, five apprentices, a bosun, sailmaker, carpenter, steward, cook and two mates (officers). The accommodation for the crew was unusual in that seamen and apprentices lived in the same deck house between the fore and main masts. It was divided into three. The fo'c'sle, where the seamen lived, was at the forward end, and immediately abaft it was the apprentices' accommodation, the galley being at the after end. The bosun, carpenter and sailmaker had cabins under the fo'c'sle head.

Captain Syviet sailed again as her master and Mr W H Mickie was appointed first mate. He was a young man of twenty-two and came from Tavistock in Devon. Besides young Bishop, Alexander H Turner, later second mate and acting first mate of the barque, J H Craig, later a second mate in the Company's barques, were also apprentices on this voyage.

The *Inversnaid* arrived at Rio de Janeiro on the 15th February, 1918, and, after discharging her coal, sailed for Wallaroo, Spencer Gulf, South Australia, in ballast on the 27th March, arriving on the 10th June. This was a popular port for apprentices for the people there, especially the girls, were kind and hospitable to the sailing ship sailors, particularly to the apprentices. Invitations for entertainments and picnics were given freely; the girls even went as far as to go on board the sailing ships to use their charms on the captains to give shore leave to the apprentices and young seamen so that they could accompany them on these most enjoyable events. I remember pleasurable picnics at Picnic Gully some years before.

Wheat in bags was loaded at Wallaroo for St John, New Brunswick, Canada, and the *Inversnaid* sailed on the 21st July, 1918. Sailing ships had then been kept out of the enemy submarine zone, as far as possible, for over a year. Cape Horn was rounded without incident and the barque was well to the northward, when, at 6.30 am on the 26th November, 1918, in latitude 30° north, longitude 53° 55′ west, she was struck by a fresh squall. Her fore topmast was sprung seven feet above the lower mast cap and was fished. It was not possible to set sail above the fore sail (the lowest sail) on the foremast, so the course was altered for Bermuda to get a new topmast. The barque was also short of fresh water. Rain water had been collected in the doldrums (a few degrees north of the equator) but salt water had got down into the fresh water tanks. Food was also short.

When the barque was approaching St George's Island, Bermuda, on the 16th December, 1918, a tug sighted her and towed her in. It was then that the crew heard of the end of the war. Commander Bishop wrote of one of the best smells he ever enjoyed in his life. It happened on the morning after the *Inversnaid* arrived at St George's Island. He was aloft unbending sail when some steak which had just come off to the barque, was being fried in the galley and the smell was wafted aloft to the yard where he was working.

Here, once again, the apprentices were given a most enjoyable time. Captain Syviet introduced them to many families ashore. It was most unusual for the people in the Island to see an ocean-going sailing ship and they did all they could to entertain the crew. Local riggers sent down the damaged fore topmast and topgallant mast and their yards, and sent up the new mast and crossed the yards again. Then the crew rigged them and bent on the sails.

Sailing orders were changed from St John to Cardiff and the barque sailed on the 23rd February, 1919, arriving on the 10th March. By then the wheat had been in the ship for nearly eight months and was beginning to sprout. The apprentices went home on leave, and when they rejoined the barque on the 30th June, they found that her name had been changed on the bows and stern to *Garthsnaid*, and her port of registry on the counter aft, to Montreal. She was now flying the Canadian Merchant Service ensign, a red ensign with the Canadian badge in the fly (the bottom corner furthest away from the flag staff). The British Admiralty had granted permission for this flag, the Canadian Red Ensign, to be worn by Canadian merchant ships on the 2nd February, 1892.

Captain Syviet had left and Captain James Simpson from Lunden Links, Fife, Scotland, aged 44, was appointed master. He had served in the Royal Naval Reserve, Trawler Section, during the war and had been awarded the Distinguished Service Cross for sinking a submarine. Before the 1914–18 war he had commanded the windjammers *Colonial Empire* and *Indian Empire* and was of the finest type of Scottish shipmaster. His wife, then aged 40, sailed with him and signed on the barque's Articles as stewardess at one shilling a month, while John Alexander Simpson, aged five, signed on as 'ship's boy' at the same rate of pay. Mr McLeod, aged 51, was the first mate and Mr Alexander Turner, aged 18, was the second mate. He had finished his apprenticeship and had passed the examination for second mate, but, being too young, was given a provisional certificate.

Seven apprentices joined on this voyage: Charles E Sanders, Joseph H Smith, Frank Bishop, Frank Newington, Edward Byrne, Richard M Sibun and Carl P Brown. G D David joined the barque later in Australia. There were only six seamen in the fo'c'sle so the accommodation was changed round and the apprentices went into the larger accommodation in the forward part of the deck house and the seamen into the after part.

Usually, in windjammers, the food for seamen and apprentices was the same; but, in George Milne's 'Inver' Line, Lady Inver had insisted that the apprentices be given a tin of fruit every week as an extra and William Garthwaite had carried on this privilege after he bought the 'Inver' line barques. That was the only sailing ship company, as far as the author knows, that gave their apprentices this luxury. A tin of condensed milk every three weeks is as near as the rest of us got to it; and, although we often drank it as soon as it was received, it was intended for tea and coffee and a type of porridge we knew as burgoo which originated with the Norsemen of the Viking Age in the eighth to the tenth centuries.

The *Garthsnaid* left Cardiff on the 1st August, 1919, with a cargo of coals for Pernambuco, Brazil, where she arrived on the 18th September. While there, Ephraim Ferguson, sailor, aged 23 from Belfast, was found ashore dead while on short shore leave. Some of the crew had the idea that he was stabbed to death, but it is obvious from the captain's report that this was not the case. Even so it will be seen that as late as 1919 there was a certain amount of risk taken by seamen who went ashore in some foreign ports. The tragedy was a mystery. The author quotes from the captain's report in the barque's 'Official Log';

> Pernambuco, 9 pm, 12.10.1919. This is to certify that E. Ferguson (sailor), with a VG [very good] character, was given [shore] leave from 6 pm, 11th October to 6 pm on the 12th October. He did not return to his ship by 8 am on Monday the 13th so I at once made enquiries. After searching all the police stations I was informed by an outsider known as 'Jack' that a British sailor had died on Sunday night and was taken to the cemetery [mortuary]. I got in touch with the police again and found that the body had been taken to the morgue at the cemetery, so I went there and found Ferguson dead [and] laid in a coffin ready for burial. I examined the body, and, as far as I could see, there had been no foul play. I at once advised the British Consul and informed him that I must have a post mortem examination on the body and a thorough inquiry made into the case. I also gave him a description of the deceased and of the man he was in company with, when last seen from the ship, on Sunday 12th [October] at 8.15 am. Until noon today, Thursday 16th, I have got no satisfaction. I have done all in my power to investigate the case but I am handicapped [in] not knowing the language; so now I leave it entirely in the hands of the British Consul.

This was signed by Captain Simpson, J McLeod, the first mate, and the Acting British Consul, Pernambuco. No further entry concerning the cause of the death of the sailor was made in the Official Log, but there was an entry concerning the effects of Ferguson being sold by auction on the main hatch. This was the practice in windjammers after the death of a member of the crew. Every piece of gear was itemised and the amount received for each article was entered in the Official Log. The auction took place at sea on the 4th May, 1920 and realised £10.4.6. This, and the wages due to Ferguson, amounting to £24.1.5, was paid to his next of kin.

After the coal cargo had been discharged the *Garthsnaid* sailed, on the 21st October, 1919, to Buenos Aires in ballast. She arrived on the 16th November. On this passage a pampero was experienced. This is a severe line squall of many hours' duration accompanied by lightning, thunder and heavy rain. All hands had a terrible night making sail fast in a hurricane force wind.

When the barque arrived she was moored at La Boca and loaded wheat; it was hoped that it would be consigned to a home port. At that time windjammers of the few maritime countries owning them were visiting Buenos Aires for wheat cargoes; and seamen serving in them were still deserting, and, some becoming beachcombers, were preying on their brother seamen who were still employed in the ships. Vice in the 'Boca' area was still thriving; the bars and prostitute-houses were still making money and doing their utmost to attract the men from the ships. 'Blue' films were being shown, pornographic books printed in English and 'dirty' postcards were being sold. Never was there more need for the good work of 'The Flying Angel Missions to Seamen', and never was better work done by them than at Buenos Aires in the last days of the windjammers. It was here that the apprentices and young seamen of the *Garthsnaid* spent their off-duty time and enjoyed their evenings and week-ends away from that part of the port which was notorious for its drunkenness and immorality. Without the entertainment and visits provided by the padres and their helpers, life in these foreign parts would have been dull and miserable for the apprentices. Although the author has mentioned the Church of England 'Missions to Seamen', other religious denominations did good work for seamen in foreign ports.

When the *Garthsnaid* received orders for her discharging port the crew were amazed and disappointed to hear that they were for Callao, Peru, which meant the dreaded east to west rounding of Cape Horn. Fortunately it was summer time in the southern hemisphere for the barque left Buenos Aires on the 10th December, 1919. She arrived at Callao on the 10th February, 1920, and although it could not be called a fast passage it was certainly shorter than made by most windjammers at that time.

There was more than Cape Horn for the Captain to contend with for only five days after the barque sailed, Frank Newington, apprentice, laid up complaining of pains in his legs and head. Captain Simpson gave him a dose of castor oil and he said he felt a bit better but remained in his bunk. But on the 19th December, he felt worse and when the captain took his temperature it was 104° Fahrenheit. He was carried aft to the saloon and put to bed in the spare room where he was under the captain's constant observation. His legs ached but he had no pains. Captain Simpson gave him a thorough examination. There was no rash. All the young apprentices could tell the captain was that he had a slight cold when the barque left Buenos Aires.

Captain Simpson then treated him for a simple fever and gave him opening medicine and the fever medicine provided in the ship's Medical Chest. He was kept on a strict milk and water diet. But after a week of this treatment young Newington showed no improvement, his temperature ranging between 101° and 104°. So Captain Simpson stopped the fever medicine and tried quinine. Still the temperature kept high and his patient was gradually getting weaker. During the third week the lad was very ill; his temperature rose to 105° and he was unable to move. He had no desire to eat so was given a little brandy and water as well as milk and water. He sweated profusely at night and the captain frequently changed his pyjamas and gave him brandy and water afterwards because he felt cold. One of his fellow apprentices stayed with him all the time at night.

As he was making no progress towards recovery Captain Simpson concluded that there might be something that was giving him a high temperature. He risked feeding him. He had no appetite and the captain started with chicken tea, egg and milk and Bovril. From that time young Newington began to get stronger and his temperature fell from 104° to 101°. On the 24th January it was normal and he was allowed to sit up for a little time. After that he continued to improve, and, although very weak, managed to get up and walk a little every day. His appetite gradually improved.

Captain Simpson reported in the 'Official Log' that during the whole of his sickness he had no pains and that there was no rash. His symptoms were high fever and sickness. When the *Garthsnaid* arrived at Callao on the 2nd February, 1920, the port doctor diagnosed the apprentice's illness as neuritis and he was sent ashore to hospital. He stayed there for eight days then returned to the ship and started work.

The apprentices seemed to be having more than their share of bad luck, for, on the 20th February, in Callao, young Sibun, whilst putting on the canvas lifeboat cover on the bridge aft, fell some eight feet to the main deck below and broke his wrist. It was set by the doctor who attended him during the barque's stay in port.

Besides the anxiety caused by the illness of young Newington, Captain Simpson had the worry of sailing the *Garthsnaid* round Cape Horn. To save distance, and to cut the mileage that had to be sailed against the strong westerly winds and gales usually experienced off Cape Horn, the captain sailed the barque through the narrow le Maire Strait—between Patagonia (Tierre del Fuego) and Staten Island in latitude 54° 48′ south. The Strait is five miles wide but a more treacherous passage would be hard to find. Tide-rips are met, and if the windjammers got too near the mainland side they were likely to meet a sudden change of wind due to its deflection from the high cliffs. And, even worse, were the sudden blasts from the 'willi-waws' that blow down the mountain sides at hurricane force and develop into off-shore whirlwinds. It was often wondered if the risks taken by sailing through this merciless Strait was worth the worry and anxiety. But the captain made the decision and it was his 'worry and anxiety'.

Sailing through the Strait, all hands stood by on deck in case a sudden shift of wind or a tide-rip should catch the barque's bow and turn her towards the beach on either side. There was an awful warning there in the shape of a big four-masted barque wrecked on Staten Island. But they went through safely, and, to their surprise, rounded Cape Horn with a fair wind. But their luck was not to hold, for, having made to the westward of Cape Horn they met a strong westerly gale which drove their barque back to the eastward, and well to the southward, thus lengthening what had promised to be a fast passage, besides adding the discomfort and hazards of a strong head gale in Cape Horn seas.

After the cargo of wheat had been discharged in Callao the *Garthsnaid* sailed to Iquique, Chile, in ballast to load nitrate. She left on the 10th March, 1920, and, although it was a short distance down the coast, the Humboldt Current flowing to the northward and the south-east trade winds lengthened the passage to twenty-five days.

In the author's time served in windjammers, less than ten years before, a nitrate cargo loaded in Chile meant a homeward passage to the United Kingdom or a European port; but trade conditions had changed and the *Garthsnaid*'s cargo was taken to Lourenço Marques in East Africa. At Iquique the barque anchored in the bay from two to three miles off shore, but no longer were there tiers of sailing ships, totalling forty or fifty, as was the case before the first world war. Neither was the old-time custom of 'Hoisting the Southern Cross', to the tune and words of the sea shanty, 'Hurrah my boys we're homeward bound', carried out. In any case, much to the disappointment of her crew, the barque was not homeward bound. It was here that Mr McLeod, the first mate, fell sick and had to be left behind.

This created a problem for there was not a certificated first mate in Iquique available. To enable the barque to sail without waiting for an officer to be sent out from Britain, Captain Simpson arranged for temporary certificates to be issued to his second mate and senior apprentice so that they could take charge of the watches in the capacity of first and second mates respectively, although it was not necessary for the second mate of a windjammer to hold a certificate at that time. The following entry was made in the 'Official Log':

> Iquique, 8th April, 1920. This is to certify that at the request of the master of the SV *Garthsnaid*, the second officer on board that vessel, Mr A Turner, was duly examined by the masters of the SV *Clackmannanshire* and the SS *Cape Fear*, both of whom hold British certificates, and found to be competent to act as first officer [mate] according to written statements handed [to] me. The present certificate is given provisionally pending the Board of Trade examination at the first possible port.

The same entry was made in regard to Apprentice H Smith, who was found competent to act as second officer (mate) by examination carried out by the same shipmasters. Apprentice Frank Bishop was promoted to third mate at this time.

It was while in Iquique that Mr Turner bought the camera with which he took the excellent bad weather photographs of scenes on deck and aloft in the *Garthsnaid*, some of which are reproduced in this book.

The barque left Iquique on the 24th April, 1920. This time a particularly bad weather passage was experienced. Down off Cape Horn a following gale of hurricane force was encountered and the only sail that could be carried was a goose-winged (half set) fore lower topsail. The team of young officers were severely tried and Captain Simpson was on the poop continuously night and day, for three days. Mrs Simpson and the steward spent most of the time making hot coffee and carrying it up to the poop deck for the captain and the officers.

When the wind eased Captain Simpson took full advantage by heaving the barque to (bringing her up to within seven points of the wind with yards braced sharp up and letting her drift to leeward with the seas). And punctured oil bags were put out forward on the weather side. The oil flattened out the tops of the seas and caused the barque to lay much quieter and without the danger of being overwhelmed. This gave the captain, his mates and the crew a much-needed rest. The orders during the three days when the barque had been running before the gale had been: 'Watch on deck stay out on deck! Watch below (off duty) keep handy!'

Off Cape Horn was not the only trying time that the crew had that passage, for rounding the Cape of Good Hope was almost as bad. This passage took 99 days to complete and on 26th July, 1920, five days before the barque reached Lourenço Marques, the fore upper topsail halliards carried away, causing the upper topsail yard to slide down the mast with such force that the lower mast cap was damaged and the fore lower topsail yard was sent crashing down on to the deck. Fortunately no one was injured.

There certainly seemed to be a 'hoodoo' on the barque at this time, for, when she arrived at her discharging port the tug's crews were on strike and Captain Simpson, with the help of the local pilot, had to sail her up to her berth. This can only be described as a clever and unusual feat of seamanship, calling for the greatest ability from a windjammer master.

Discharging the nitrate was a slow job and there was difficulty in getting ballast for the barque to make her next passage to Newcastle, Australia, to load coal. At least the apprentices were not impatient to leave for they were invited on board the Union Castle passenger liners and the Clan Line cargo liners for meals. Repairs were carried out and when the barque left on the 24th September, she was in as good a condition as could be expected for her age.

The passage across the South Indian Ocean was made between latitudes 40° and 45° south. On the 15th October, 1920, at 1 am, when the *Garthsnaid* was running wildly before a strong westerly gale, she broached-to. She rolled terrifically with a quick, sharp, movement. Fortunately nothing carried away, and after the yards were hauled round she was put on course again with no damage or casualties. It was lucky, for it was not unusual for a windjammer, when broached-to, to roll right over on to her side and sometimes the only way to get her to return to the upright was to cut her masts and let them fall over the side.

This passage took 49 days and Newcastle was not reached until the 11th November, 1920. During the passage Mr Smith, the acting second mate, and Mr Bishop the third mate, finished their apprenticeship and the former was signed on the ship's Articles at £18 a month and the latter at £14.10s a month. Later when Carl Brown completed his apprenticeship he was signed on as an able seaman at £14.10s a month. Just over four years before when I finished my apprenticeship in a British windjammer, I was signed on as able seaman at £2.10s a month.

Newcastle was always a favourite port with the men serving in sailing ships, because, apart from the friendliness and hospitality of the Australian people, there was at Stockton one of the most popular 'Missions to Seamen' in any part of the world. When I first went there it was a corrugated iron building. The Rev W Forster Haire, who was a sailing ship apprentice and officer before taking Holy Orders, his charming wife and lovely young daughter and the helpers, both girls and men, were the finest team of entertainers of seamen that the author met in his time in windjammers. The Mission launch *Ada* was always available to take the apprentices and seamen ashore if their ships were anchored or at the buoys in the Hunter River. And if no shore leave could be granted the 'Mission' people would come off to the ships bringing the most delicious cakes—I still remember those attractive Victoria Sandwiches cooked by Mrs Haire—and provide such a tea as could never be obtained on board. On occasions they brought their harmonium on board and held a service. Then there were the picnics up the Hunter River, and the much enjoyed visits to the beautiful house and gardens of Mrs Castleden of Toronto on Lake Macquarie. After sixty years the author still prizes an autograph album containing entries from the girls at the 'Mission'.

Stan Hugill, who was serving in the last of the fleet, the *Garthpool*, when she was wrecked, and whose experiences will be related later, has written an excellent book with the title *Sailortown*'. He devotes several pages to Newcastle, New South Wales, describing in detail the seamy side of the port including Big Nelly Norman's Boarding House from which sailors were shipped on board outward bound sailing ships when dead drunk, and the famous pubs 'Clarendon' and 'Black Diamond' and their well-known barmaids. These, and other pubs, were frequented by sailors from the windjammers and the 'ladies' who befriended them. Stan has also something to say about the 'Missions to Seamen' which I endorse heartily:

> But over at Stockton, pretty little Stockton, where the ships went to discharge their ballast, life was more pleasant for sailormen. The 'Missions to Seamen' there was known to all sailormen, and, since it had its own launch pleasant, rosy-cheeked Mission girls would be brought over nightly to entertain the lads from the ballast ships [windjammers.] Dances and concerts and whist drives all helped 'Deep Water John' to forget his arduous sea life, and many an apprentice left Newcastle with his heart in the keeping of some sweet young Mission girl. [Oh how true!]

In 1912 the old 'Tin Mission' was wrecked by the 'Great Storm' late one Sunday afternoon when eighty men and boys were present from the windjammers. They were having tea when the water from the harbour came surging in to the Mission. The seamen and the apprentices had the enjoyable privilege of carrying their favourite girls out to safety. £5,800 was raised to build a new Mission and a fine brick building was erected opposite the North Stockton Ferry, complete with the chapel and chaplain's house.

Mr Haire was chaplain at Newcastle for nine years and was transferred to the Antwerp Mission in 1923. He spent his last years in a cottage on the Undercliffe near Ventnor in the Isle of Wight. The author feels he must repeat an extract from a letter he received from Mr Haire, shortly before he died, which was quoted in *The Wheel's Kick and the Wind's Song*.

> The old Stockton Mission (Newcastle, New South Wales) was our life's work, and I feel now rather like a poor old sailorman hauled ashore for good, and longing for the smell of ropes and Stockolm tar again.

If ever a man was a sailor's friend that man was the Rev W Forster Haire; his name is still revered and remembered with affection by all who sailed in the last of the windjammers.

While the *Garthsnaid* was in Newcastle on this occasion the British sailing ships, *Monkbarns*, *Vimiera* and *Kirkcudbrightshire* were there as well as the pretty little New Zealand barques *Raupo* and *Rauno*. Here, Mr Frederick Kane, aged 38, of Belfast, who had a certificate as first mate, joined the *Garthsnaid* in that capacity and Mr Turner resumed his original rank of second mate. Mr Smith, who had been second mate, having finished his apprenticeship, left for home.

The *Garthsnaid* left Newcastle with a cargo of coals on the 14th December, 1920, for Iquique, Chile, and made a long passage of 83 days, during which time the crew celebrated their second Christmas at sea in the barque. The old windjammer method of discharging the coal in baskets, and heaving them out of the hold by hand with dolly winches, was carried out in the *Garthsnaid*, although Messrs A D Bordes' beautiful French barques were there using steam winches for discharging and loading and were doing the job in half the time. Mr Sibun remembers four of the famous German 'P' line sailing ships still lying in the bay at anchor from the time they were interned there early in the 1914–18 war. Their anchor cables and hulls were thick with sea grass and barnacles. The chains of the cables were two inches in diameter with marine growth, and the barnacles on the ships' sides were so large that it was possible to stand on them.

There was no cargo at Iquique for the *Garthsnaid*, so she took in ballast and sailed for Sydney, Australia, on the 18th April, 1922. She had now been away from Britain for two years without going into dry dock to get her bottom cleaned and painted and was showing a slowing up in her sailing speed. On this passage she sailed across the South Pacific in about latitude 20° south and did not arrive in Sydney until the 22nd July; a lengthy passage of 94 days. Although slow it was a pleasant passage in glorious weather all the way. The south-east trade winds could have been stronger to cut the passage time, but those on board remember the sunrises and sunsets as the most beautiful they have ever seen. On one occasion the *Garthsnaid* was becalmed for nearly a week, and drifting near to her was an American whaler barque. She reported a good haul and holds full. Later it was learnt that she had been lost with all hands near the entrance to San Francisco Harbour.

The *Garthsnaid* was dry-docked at North Woolwich, Sydney, before she loaded wheat in bags at Pyrmont for Falmouth for orders. Mr Kane, the first mate, left here and Mr Ernest F Letts, aged 35, took his place at £24 a month! (Ten years before, the first mate's pay in windjammers sailing out of London was £9 a month.) He was said to be an excellent officer and seaman and held a first mate's, square-rigged certificate. He was educated at Whitgift School, Croydon, had been a rubber planter in Malaya and spoke several Far Eastern languages. He had served in the Australian army in the First World War.

The *Garthsnaid* sailed from Sydney on the 20th August, 1921. To prepare for sailing she went to anchor. On the early morning of her sailing day she was surrounded by yachts and launches, their crews joining in the capstan shanties while her crew were heaving up the anchor. Unfortunately there was an unrehearsed event which marred the historic procedure. When the anchor cable was still leading slightly ahead from the barque's hawse pipe, and the crew were pushing the capstan bars round the capstan with all their strength to break out the anchor from the bottom of the harbour, the first mate shouted to the tug to go ahead slow to take the weight off the anchor and help the crew heaving on the capstan. The tug went ahead too quickly and one of the pawls of the capstan (they are fitted to prevent the capstan running back) broke, and the other pawls jumped. The capstan ran back and scattered the crew who were heaving on the capstan bars, throwing some of them against the fo'c'sle head rails, and others overboard. Launches were quickly on the spot to pick them out of the water. The injuries received were minor ones: all the same it spoilt the show.

Captain Simpson took the *Garthsnaid* well south to latitude 50° for the wind when crossing the South Pacific to Cape Horn. When crossing the meridian of longitude 162° west, the barque was in latitude 53° south. Strong westerly gales were experienced and the half deck and fo'c'sle, in the forward deck house, were continually flooded. The weather was unbearably cold with snow and ice as it was, of course, winter time. It lasted for forty days until the barque was to the northward of the Falkland Islands in the South Atlantic. Not only was the weather bitterly cold, but, down there in the fifties, the nights were terribly long and there was little daylight. The apprentices and seamen were unable to sleep in their bunks which had been washed out by the seas that had smashed into the house. All their clothes were wet and there was no place to dry them. The galley was flooded out most of the time, and on many days there was no hot food. Their only consolation was that every day was one nearer home.

At 3.45 pm on the 15th September, 1921, came the most tragic happening of the voyage. The 'Official Log' gives the briefest possible description:

> 15.9.21. 3.45 pm. Latitude 51° 55′ south, longitude 114° 15′ west. Blowing a heavy south-westerly gale with mountainous seas running, ship under foresail, lower topsails and main upper topsail, and shipping tremendous quantities of water. Whilst Sanders, apprentice, was coming aft to strike the bell [one bell] at a quarter to four pm,

ship [barque] shipped a huge sea and washed him overboard; owing to weather conditions we were unable to render him any assistance whatever.

(signed) J Simpson, master
Edmund S F Letts, mate
E Long, boatswain [bosun]
R Sibun, apprentice.

More details were given to the author by Charles Sanders' fellow apprentices serving in the *Garthsnaid* at the time. They reported that a heavy sea crashed on board on the main deck in the waist of the ship, lifted him up and washed him overboard before he had a chance of grabbing anything to hold on to. The captain and first mate were both on the poop at the time and saw him go overboard. He was last seen in the wake of the ship, on the surface of the mountainous seas, waving his arms. It was not possible to put one of the lifeboats over the side into the sea, in fact it would have been dangerous to attempt to bring the barque up into the wind and sea to make it possible for a boat to be launched. Even if it had been launched without being smashed against the side of the barque, or capsized, it would have been an almost impossible job for the barque to pick the boat up again. There were the lives of the volunteers in the boat to consider. The captain had to make the decision; and it was a terrible one to have to make, especially as he knew there would be no lack of volunteers to risk their lives in an attempt to rescue their shipmate. It cast gloom and depression over all hands for Charlie Sanders was well liked by everyone on board.

A memorial service was held in the saloon in the second dog-watch (6 pm to 8 pm) that evening which all hands attended except the man on the look-out, the man at the wheel and the officer in charge of the watch, Mrs Simpson played the hymns on the cabin harmonium.

Charlie Sanders had started his sea career late in life. He came from Petersfield in Hampshire and was twenty-seven years of age when he was lost at sea. He had served in the British Army as an officer right through the 1914–1918 war, and in 1919 decided to start a new career at sea as an apprentice and signed indentures when he was twenty-five years of age. He was a fine shipmate liked by all on board. Mr Letts, the first mate, who was a soldier and a sailor himself was impelled to write:

A Sacrifice to Duty

Blow up, blow out you gallant west'ly winds,
Check not your anger, but let your passions free,
Homeward we're bound, 'tis true we hope to find
Sweethearts, wives and mothers waiting for you, for me.

Like a hound unleashed the little barque sails on,
Tearing her path through foaming, crested seas,
A crack, a roar, another sail has gone,
A sacrifice to you oh bold and valiant breeze,

Strong blows the gale and showing meagre sail,
Her decks awash, seas thundering fore and aft,
The little barque runs hard before the gale,
A noble sight, a staunch and gallant craft.

But hark! A cry is heard above the crash and moan:
'Man overboard!' Oh Christ it cannot be!
Not in a gale like this; not left to fight alone
In such a raging, vast and lonely sea!

'Tis true! Look to the foaming yeastly wake and sea,
A feeble hand is raised in last appeal,
Poor human atom! Helpless both you and me;
No boat could live, so on the barque must sail.

No tombstone there to mark your sleeping head;
No flowers bud forth in spring upon your grave;
A sacrifice to duty 'neath the cold and silent wave.

Shipmate! In the day of reckoning yet to come
Fearless and upright you at least can stand,
Soldier and sailor you answered duties call,
A credit to your flag and native land.

E Letts,
1st Mate, barque *Garthsnaid*
South Pacific, 15th September, 1921.

The *Garthsnaid* continued her eastward run and early on the morning of the 25th September, the islands and rocks of the Diego Ramirez, some 60 miles to the south-west of Cape Horn, were sighted. The wind and sea had moderated and now a strong south-westerly wind and good visibility favoured the barque. Cape Horn was sighted at 6.30 am, deeply covered in snow. The *Garthsnaid* was thirty-six days out from Sydney. Then came the run to the northward in the South Atlantic. The weather improved and the sun came out to dry the fo'c'sle and half deck and clothes that felt dry and warm were put on once again.

The equator was crossed on the 30th October in longitude 30° west when the barque was 71 days out from Sydney. By the 17th November she had arrived in latitude 33° north, longitude 37° west and the Italian steamer *Adanello* altered course to pass her close and promised to report her to Lloyd's. But good luck did not continue. On the next day a head wind was encountered which drove the barque back 18 miles. Then, on the 20th November, a northerly gale made it essential for sail to be reduced right down to lower topsails and she was driven back again to the southward.

On the 4th December the barque was only 450 miles from Falmouth and two days later Bishop's Rock Light, Scilly Islands, was sighted from the main royal yard at 9.30 pm. Off the Lizard William Watkin's London tug *Hibernia* took her in tow to Falmouth where she anchored in Carrick Roads at noon on the 7th December after an excellent passage of 109 days from Iquique. It was the best sailing ship passage made at that time, the next best being one of 114 days by a French sailing ship.

Orders were received to discharge the cargo at Bristol and she was towed round to the port on the 14th December, 1921. Whilst she was being towed up the Bristol Channel the wind increased to a south-westerly gale and Captain Simpson decided to set sail to help the tug. She overran the tug which had to slip the tow-rope. The tug picked the barque up again off the entrance to the River Avon. When towing up river, and negotiating the difficult Horse Shoe Bend, the tow rope carried away and the barque nearly ran ashore on the river bank. Fortunately the tug got her tow rope on board the barque quickly and towed her up river under the Clifton Suspension Bridge to the entrance to the City Docks. She was moored at a berth near the Centre where her jib boom slanted up over the road and the traffic passed underneath it.

The crew paid off on the 17th December, 1921, after a voyage of two years, four months, and seventeen days. Byrne and Sibun were the only two apprentices who had not finished their apprenticeship and they, after only ten days' leave, had to return to the barque.

Chapter Four

The *Garthsnaid's* last voyage

After the grain was discharged at Bristol the *Garthsnaid* was towed across the Bristol Channel to Port Talbot on the 11th February, 1922, to load patent fuel for Port Louis, Mauritius. Coastwise Articles were opened for this short passage. The master was Captain W G Churchill, and the name and address of the owners were: The Marine Navigation Company, Montreal, 5 Lloyds Avenue, London EC. In the foreign-going Articles for the next voyage the same name and address was given; the port of registry on the stern of the ship was still Montreal.

Captain Simpson had left the barque and Captain John Roberts, aged 55, of St David's, Pembroke, Wales, took over the command for the next voyage. Mr Letts signed on again as first mate, and Richard Sibun, still serving his apprenticeship, acted as second mate. Edward Byrne was promoted to third mate and three new apprentices joined the barque; they were A G Leckie of Edinburgh, who came from the barque *Hougomont*, A W Merrick of the USA from the *Vimiera* and E S MacPherson of Sydney, Australia.

Seamen with experience in windjammers were now hard to find and some signed on for this voyage who had never served in sailing ships before. It does seem that the *Garthsnaid* was undermanned in this respect for there were only four experienced able seamen, and two of those were 50 and 60 years old, two sailors and two ordinary seamen, although the latter had served in windjammers. In spite of this they proved a reliable crew when called on in a difficult and dangerous situation early in the voyage.

While the barque was at Port Talbot, the owner, Sir William Garthwaite, Bart, came on board to make a personal survey and pay a call on the Captain and officers. He was then forty-seven years of age but Captain J M Hood, a New Zealander, who had just joined the barque as an ordinary seaman, described him as a smartly dressed young man in his thirties. He looked more like a bank manager then a sailing ship owner; but, in spite of his appearance, it was obvious that he knew a great deal about windjammers and he took a great interest in the barque's gear as well as her crew. Young Hood had served two and a half years in the full-rigged ship *Mount Stewart* which he had joined at Melbourne and paid off from at Cardiff. He had found life in the fo'c'sle unbearable and wanted to get his four years' service completed in sail as soon as possible so that he could sit for a second mate's square-rigged certificate. While it is true that some of the men who served in the fo'c'sle of windjammers were uncouth and unpleasant there was a great improvement in them, as time went on, in the ships and barques of Sir William Garthwaite. This was particularly noticeable in the last voyage of the *Garthforce*. The other ordinary seaman in the *Garthsnaid*, on this voyage, was a good type of youth named Tommy Oxham, from Vancouver, Canada.

The *Garthsnaid* was towed to sea from Port Talbot docks on Friday, the 3rd March, 1922, on a cold winter's morning. Captain Roberts was obviously not as superstitious as the masters the author served under for they would not sail on Friday. As soon as the barque cleared the lock the lower staysails were set to a light fair wind. But before she had cleared the Bristol Channel the wind went round and freshened to a south-westerly gale. Then the tow rope got foul across the barque's bow and it was slipped from the tug which then turned and ran back to Port Talbot. Sail had to be set as quickly as possible, and when it came to hoisting the upper topsail yards it was found that it was all both watches could do to hoist one yard by hand.

The tow rope was taken in by the capstan and then followed a hazardous, hard night with all hands staying on deck to wear ship (put her round on the other tack) every three or four hours. At the end of every inshore run Lundy Island Light seemed nearer to the crew, but it must be said in their favour, that, by daylight they had become an efficient team in their struggle to claw off the land. It took three days to clear the entrance to the Bristol Channel. On Tuesday the wind veered to the north-west and increased in strength to force ten, necessitating the barque's sail to be reduced to lower topsails and the barque to be hove-to. When the gale eased up the wind settled from the north and gave the barque a fair wind out into the North Atlantic.

She picked up the north-east trade winds in the latitude of Madeira, and, after passing through the doldrums with their heavy rains and variable winds, met the south-east trades to the northward of the equator and sailed southward with them until the westerly winds were picked up in about latitude 30° south. They developed into strong winds and later the weather became heavily overcast so that no altitudes of the sun could be taken to fix the barque's position with reasonable accuracy. Visibility decreased as the barque drove south and east until murky, swirling mists reduced it to about a mile.

It was the practice of windjammer masters to set a course to sight Tristan da Cunha, for, not only was it on their track for South African or Australian ports, it also helped to check the rate of the gaining or losing of their chronometers by giving them an exact longitude. The *Garthsnaid* had had to be navigated by dead reckoning, and Captain Roberts kept his look-outs going in the daytime as well as at night when, by his calculation, the barque was nearing Tristan da Cunha.

One afternoon, when the barque was running before a strong breeze with all sail set to topgallant sails, and when young Leckie, the Scottish apprentice was on the look-out, he suddenly gave a terrific shout: 'Land right ahead!' The wheel was put up immediately, all hands ran to the braces and the barque bore away from the danger. Captain Roberts had seen enough of it to identify the peak as that of Tristan da Cunha, and he had obtained his correct position to set his course for rounding the Cape of Good Hope.

The *Garthsnaid* arrived at Port Louis on the 4th June, 1922, after a passage of 93 days. She was moored at the buoys and the cargo of patent fuel in briquettes, each a little longer than a brick, was hoisted out of the holds by means of a dolly winch. The natives helped at the dolly winch on deck and sang their calypsos, to give the time for winding, in quaint old English. They were stories of their everyday lives. The crew could not resist joining in the choruses.

Here the younger seamen, apprentices and officers played football ashore; especially at week-ends. The army garrison were stationed at a point near the *Garthsnaid*'s moorings and they allowed the crew full use of their football ground. Matches were arranged between the crew of the barque and the garrison, and at times against crews of visiting steamers. Unfortunately, Mr Letts, the first mate, broke his leg while playing, and the young third mate Edward Byrne who was only seventeen and a half years of age, took charge of his watch for the next passage to Australia.

While the ship was at the buoys in Port Louis the apprentices and ordinary seamen started evening navigation classes under the fo'c'sle head. Empty salt meat casks, sawn into halves, served as tables, and upturned buckets did duty as chairs. Lighting was provided with hurricane lamps, a special allowance of kerosine oil being supplied by Captain Roberts. Every evening the nautical students struggled with *Nicholl's Guide*. What a difference there is now with the excellent nautical schools ashore which give pre-sea training, mid-apprenticeship coaching and preparation for the examinations from second mate to extra master. There were, of course, in the days of the windjammers, good schools, mostly for cramming, which prepared candidates for the examinations, but nothing in comparison with those which are available today. In many ships nowadays special cabins are provided for study; and there are the invaluable Merchant Navy Training Board and Correspondence Courses run from Nautical Schools. Of course, examinations have become increasingly more difficult to pass and there is now a University degree open to Merchant Navy officers.

When the cargo had been discharged at Port Louis, sand ballast was taken on board, trimmed level in the lower holds and then covered with stones on top of which boards were spread. The whole was tommed down and then lashed down with lengths of chain and mooring lines. On this passage the barque was certain to roll and pitch heavily in the bad weather and the work carried out to prevent the ballast shifting and sending the barque over on to her beam ends was well repaid. In the event the weather was not too bad. Orders were received for Port Phillip, Melbourne, where the crew hoped that wheat would be loaded for a home port. The *Garthsnaid* sailed from Port Louis on the 3rd August, 1922, and brought up to anchor off Queenscliff, Port Phillip Bay, on the 7th September, 1922. She had made the passage in 35 days.

Sixteen days were spent at anchor before orders came to sail direct to Iquique in Chile. Obviously there was no wheat available. In the author's time in windjammers there was always a coal cargo to load at Newcastle, New South Wales, for a port on the west coast of South America. It seems hard to believe that the *Garthsnaid* would have been sent across the South Pacific in ballast if a freight-paying cargo had been available. One thing was certain; cargoes for windjammers were becoming harder to get. Their last days were fast approaching.

While the barque was waiting for orders off Queenscliff an unusual method was adopted for filling the fresh water tanks. Either no fresh water boat was available or it was a matter of economy. The second mate was put in charge of one of the boats and a large empty tank was landed on, and lashed across her thwarts. There was no room for the crew of the boat to row so she had to be sailed. Buckets were filled with fresh water from a stand-pipe ashore, carried to the boat and emptied into the tank. The boat was then sailed back to the barque where the tank was hoisted on board with a tackle rigged to the main yard arm. Then another empty tank was lowered into the boat, and, while the boat was sailed to the shore to get it filled, the fresh water in the first full tank was transferred to the ship's tank on board. This is something new to the author who remembers that while moored to a wooden jetty in Guayaquil, Ecuador, a gang of three, of which he was one, pushed empty salt beef barrels on a trolley to a tap in the Gas Works yard, filled them with buckets and then pushed the loaded trolley back to the ship and poured the buckets of water into the fresh water tanks on board. This was carried out in the hot weather of a port two degrees from the equator. The hours worked were from six o'clock in the morning till six o'clock at night, every day of the week except Sunday, for six weeks. No doubt it was economical for I understood that the water was given to the ship and I know that the three workers were unpaid.

The *Garthsnaid* left Queenscliff for Iquique on the 23rd September, 1922. Mr Letts was fit again and took charge of his watch. The barque experienced the same series of westerly gales down in the roaring forties, but, sailing in ballast, she was high out of the water, and shipped little water on to her decks. But in spite of this another tragedy occurred, not far from the place where Charlie Sanders lost his life on the previous voyage. It took place on the 12th October, 1922, when the *Garthsnaid* was running before a gale of wind under lower topsails and foresail at about nine knots. There was a very high sea running. The report in the 'Official Log' reads:

> 12.10.22, latitude 50° 40′ south, longitude 173° west. This is to certify that on the 12th October, 1922, blowing a moderate gale from north-north-west, at 3.15 pm hauled down the inner jib, and, after making the sail fast, T Oxham, ordinary seaman, who had been assisting two able seamen, went out [on jib boom] to tighten the gaskets on the outer jib. Whilst doing this he slipped backwards [off the footrope] and fell overboard [into the sea]. The wash of the ship carried him clear of the bow and clear of the ship's side. A lifebuoy was thrown to him and reached within a few yards of him. He made no attempt to reach it and appeared to be sinking. He was unable to swim. All hands were called immediately, hauled up the foresail and hauled down the staysails, and the ship was brought close to the wind. By this time the lifebuoy was well to windward and the second officer, Mr Sibun, who was up the mizzen rigging, reported that he could only see the lifebuoy and S R Slade, able seaman, saw the man sinking. All hands were consulted and it was decided that it would not be safe to launch the lifeboat and [the crew of the lifeboat] would not be able to pull to windward towards the lifebuoy.
>
> (signed) John Roberts, master
> Edmund E F Letts, chief officer
> S R Slade, able seaman.

Tommy Oxham, it will be remembered, came from Vancouver, Canada. He was eighteen years of age.

The *Garthsnaid* arrived at Iquique on the 12th November, 1922, after making a passage of 47 days. The ballast was discharged by the crew, and the nitrate was hauled on board by them, but the actual stowage was carried out by one Chilian stevedore. The heavy bags—they weighed about two hundredweight—were landed on a stage of bags underneath the hatchway where the stevedore took one at a time on his back, carried it to the position of stowage, and dropped it in position with an exactitude that was amazing. At the bottom of the hold the bags went right across the full width of the barque, and each successive layer or row was less in width as the stowage rose. The bags were built up in pyramid shape. This was done to increase the height of the bags in the hold to raise the weight in order to give the barque the type of stability necessary for the bad weather and heavy seas she would surely encounter.

One thing was seen during the *Gathsnaid*'s stay in Iquique that confirmed stories that, on occasions, windjammers missed their ports of arrival altogether and were swept to the north by the current. The Humboldt Current runs to the northward along the coast and sailing ships must sail in boldly towards the coast to a point to the southward of their port to make sure of sailing into it. A big French four-masted barque was seen approaching Iquique one morning and by noon she was about three miles off the anchorage but was being swept to the northward. When she did brace up her yards on the starboard tack to run into the anchorage the south-east trade winds did not give her enough speed to overcome the leeway she was making and the north-setting current. The small tug *Emu* steamed out to her assistance and put her tow rope on board, but she was unable to tow her in and eventually had to let go the tow rope. The barque was carried away to the northward. There was only one thing that her master could do; steer straight out to sea until the current was cleared, then make to the southward of Iquique and have another try. This he did but it was a month before his barque was sighted again by the ships in Iquique, and this time he did sail her into the anchorage.

The *Garthsnaid* loaded her nitrate for Melbourne which meant a passage across the South Pacific in the fine weather of the south-east trade winds. In the event they were lighter than usual and there were far more calms and rain squalls than the crew liked. The long passage made them run short of food, and they ran completely out of tobacco.

On the 28th February, 1923, Mr R M Sibun, acting second mate, finished his apprenticeship and his wages were, from that date, £10 a month. This seems quite wrong to me because, on a previous voyage, when Frank Bishop, who was then third mate, finished his apprenticeship, he was paid £14.10s a month, and C P M Brown, who was signed on as an able seaman, was also paid at the rate of £14.10s a month, having finished his apprenticeship. I took this information from the barque's official papers, and can only conclude that the terms in the apprentices' indentures were worded differently as regards the pay.

To get back to the passage of the *Garthsnaid* across the Pacific; the soft days of the fine weather were to end suddenly, dramatically, and quite unexpectedly. The 'Official Log' gives the most reliable report of the catastrophe, and that will be quoted first. But the experiences and impressions of the second mate and able seaman Hood—he had been promoted during the voyage—are far too important to be omitted. The 'Official Log' reported:

> March 30th, 1923, 4.30 pm latitude 39° 26′ south, longitude 144° 6′ east. This is to certify that on March 30th, 1923 [Good Friday] at 4.30 pm, the main starboard topmast backstay carried away, also [the] topgallant and royal backstay, and, before anything could be done, the main topgallant mast went over to port and [on the] next roll the topmast and yards went over to starboard; the fore topgallant mast and yards carried away [at] the same time. The mainmast now went over to starboard, buckling over about four feet from the deck, and again fell over [on] to the starboard bulwarks. All wreckage was cut away at midnight [and] the main mast broke off at the rail [topgallant bulwarks]. We then cut the main stay and all the wreckage went clear. Two boats were smashed and one [was] damaged. At the time of the accident it was blowing a very heavy gale from west-south-west and a very heavy sea [was running]. The ship was under two lower topsails at the time the first of the rigging carried away. As soon as the weather moderated I steered for Gabo Island Light [south-east point of Victoria, Australia] so as to get in the track of the steamers. Sunday, 1st April, the SS *Zealandic* came alongside [and] I asked him [the captain] to take us in tow to Melbourne. After several attempts to get the hawser of the *Zealandic*

on board at 5.30 pm [we] secured [the] hawser and started to tow.
(signed) John Roberts, master
R M Sibun, acting 2nd mate.

Mr Sibun attributes the start of the trouble to a Southerly Buster which hit the barque 70 miles south-south-east of Gabo Island. The barque was immediately shortened down to lower topsails and she was hove-to. She then rolled heavily in an angry sea. Mr Sibun was lying in his bunk when he heard a sharp crack, followed immediately by the blowing of three whistles for all hands on deck. One of the starboard backstays had carried away near the main deck and the watch on deck had rigged up a tackle on the backstay doubling, and were taking it to the after capstan to heave it tight, when the barque gave a sudden very heavy lurch and the other starboard backstays carried away with a succession of reports. Mr Letts and some of the crew ran forward and Mr Sibun and the remainder ran aft as the main royal and topgallant mast, yards and gear fell from aloft and crashed to leeward. This was followed by the main topmast, the heel of the topmast being suspended from the main top. Shortly after the main mast broke off about four feet above the main deck and all that had remained aloft fell over the starboard side and was towed alongside the barque held by the shrouds and backstays that were still attached to the deck. The fore topgallant mast had been dragged down by the stays attached to the main mast and was battering the fore topsail, and the mizzen topmast had also crashed down.

Captain Hood, then an able seaman on board, gave the author an apt description of his feelings:

'Then the mainmast started to carry away. Before our stunned yet fascinated eyes a strange scene of unreality took place. All that elaborate fabric of masts, yards and rigging that had become part of our lives, and as indestructible as the Rock of Gibraltar, was slowly but steadily falling into the water. Within an hour the ruin was complete and only the fore lower mast with its fore yard and two topsail yards, and the mizzen mast [lower mast] remained.

The urgent need now was to cut away the wreckage as quickly as

> possible. We could hear the steel yard arms [ends] overside thudding ominously against the barque's side as she rolled in the troughs of the heavy seas. The dismasting had taken less than an hour; the cutting away of the wreckage of masts, yards and gear took twenty-four hours. The heaviest job of all was to get the main lower mast clear over the side. As it sank it took most of the tangled wreckage, that had been cluttered round the deck, with it.

All the cutting tools available were handed out to the crew, axes, saws, cold chisels, topmauls—everything that would cut or break. Again it was proved that hitting the box screws of the rigging with heavy topmauls would not 'cut away' the backstays and shrouds.

Seas washed across the decks with great force making it difficult for the crew to keep on their feet while blocks and wires were hurled in all directions by the pitching and rolling of the barque, threatening everybody in their path. It was a non-stop job with no time for meals. In this highly dangerous job Mr Sibun, the young acting second mate, led the seamen and apprentices. Captain Roberts, dazed with the apparent impossibility of it all, stayed on deck the whole time directing operations. During this time Mr Letts went below into the holds to make a thorough examination and reported that the ship's side had not been holed. The two lifeboats had been so badly damaged that they were useless and the pipe to the fresh water tanks had been broken off and the tanks filled with salt water. A section of the starboard bulwarks had been battered down by the falling mainmast.

The dangerous job of lashing the fore topgallant mast to the fore topmast to prevent it falling from aloft was carried out and then the foresail and fore lower topsail were set, the yards squared, and the barque run before the wind towards the coast. Even with this small amount of sail set, which gave her a speed of only two knots, she was more comfortable and the rolling and pitching was less.

On Sunday morning, the 2nd April, at 2 am, a steamer's lights were sighted, and, in answer to the barque's distress signals, she altered course to go to her assistance. She was the White Star cargo liner *Zealandic*,

10,898 tons gross, bound from Sydney to Geelong (Melbourne). She agreed to tow the barque to Melbourne. At dawn, her second mate came over to the barque in one of the steamer's boats with a two-inch line. In the boat was a large package of tobacco and cigarettes and a keg of fresh water, but the sea was too rough to enable the water to be got on board. The crew, worn out with continuous work, and having had little food, had to tackle the difficult and heavy task of their share of getting the towing gear connected to the *Zealandic*.

The first job was to heave 30 fathoms of anchor cable out of the chain locker and fleet it along the deck ready for paying it out of the hawse pipe in the barque's bow. Then the steamer's towing wire was hove on board with the capstan on the fo'c'sle head and shackled on to the cable which was slacked away until it brought up on the windlass and the brake applied to hold it. Stoppers (lengths of rope) and wire preventers were set up on the cable on the fore side of the windlass to take as much weight off it as possible. Then the *Zealandic* went ahead and the towing wire and cable tautened. But the cable whipped up out of the sea so quickly, and with such force, that the stoppers and preventers snapped, putting a sudden weight on the windlass which the brake could not hold. The whole of the cable then came tearing up out of the chain locker and fell to the bottom of the sea.

The crew of the *Zealandic* hove their towing wire in until they came to the shackle connecting it with the cable; then they disconnected it from the wire and allowed the whole 120 fathoms of starboard cable to fall to the sea bed. The whole of the work had to be repeated; this time with the barque's port cable. The brake of the windlass was not trusted on this occasion and the cable was made fast to the forward mooring bitts and round the foremast at fore deck level. A tackle, consisting of two treble sheave blocks and a new 3½-inch manilla rope, was also made fast to the anchor cable to ease any sudden strains to which it might be subjected.

Before the *Zealandic* towed the barque through the entrance at Port Phillip Heads the tow-rope had to be shortened to give the steamer more control of her tow. This was done by taking the anchor cable back on to the barque's windlass and heaving it in. It was then made fast to the windlass.

Towing through the 'rip' at the entrance to the Bay the *Garthsnaid* took a sudden sheer away from the *Zealandic*, and the extra strain on the towing gear tore the holding bolts of the windlass out of the deck and dragged it, badly damaged, to the hawse pipe where it jammed and effectively held the cable. It was impossible for the barque to anchor so the *Zealandic* towed her to Hobson's Bay where the Melbourne tug *James Patterson* took over and put her alongside the Railway Pier for the discharge of her cargo which was destined for the Lyall Chemical Works. The salvage award made to the *Zealandic* was £6,350.

The *Garthsnaid* was declared a Total Constructive Loss and after her cargo was discharged she was sold to a local firm and towed to Yarrowville. She ended her days as a coal hulk and the crew were sent back to Britain as Distressed British Seamen. Captain Roberts, Mr Byrne, the third mate, and the apprentices Leckie and Merrick sailed to England in the P & O passenger liner, RMS *Naldera.* Young Byrne finished his apprenticeship on the way home in the liner. In August 1934, he visited Melbourne in command of the *British Chemist* and spent several hours alone on board the old *Garthsnaid* just walking round the decks reliving the old days he served on board. He wrote: 'I suppose I must have been very fond of her.'

Two years later, in 1936, it was reported that the owners' representatives of the hulk had refused to carry out the Harbour Master's orders to remove her. It was said that she had then been lying at South Wharf more than three years and £1,076 was outstanding on her for harbour dues, which was far in excess of her value.

As far as the author can ascertain the *Garthsnaid* was broken up in Melbourne in the 1940s.

The *Wray Castle*

The *Wray Castle*, later to have her name changed to the *Garthwray*, was a three-masted, full-rigged ship of 1,791 tons register, built in 1889 by R Williamson of Workington for J Chambers of Liverpool. She was sold to J B Walmsley & Company of Liverpool in 1899 and they sold her to R Thomas & Company, also of Liverpool, in 1911 for £3,600. The Marine Navigation Company of Canada (William Garthwaite) bought her on the 27th August, 1917. In the Articles of Agreement (with the crew) of her coastwise passage from Plymouth to Newport, Mon, which were opened on the 22nd August, 1917, and closed on the 2nd September, 1917, she was entered as being owned by The Marine Navigation Company Limited of 92/94 Gracechurch Street, London EC. Captain W Sharp was entered as master and J R Wylde as first mate.

When the *Wray Castle* was bought by Mr Garthwaite the whalers at South Georgia were short of coal while whale oil was urgently needed in Britain for the manufacture of munitions, so the ship loaded a full cargo of coal for Grytricken, South Georgia Island, close to the Antartic. Mr Garthwaite was looking for an experienced master for her, and his friend Mr Young of the London sailing ship owners, John Stewart & Company, recommended Captain Martin Frampton. At the interview in London, in August, 1917, the Captain asked first if his wife could sail with him in the *Wray Castle*. Permission was given. Mr Garthwaite described Mrs Frampton as a 'demure, refined little lady, nicely turned out, who would have done credit to any tea-party given at the vicarage of a country parson'. She asked for a plan of the ship so that she could see the captain's accommodation. When she saw that the ship had a chart house on the poop deck she agreed that her husband should accept the command. 'It has been the dream of my life,' she said, 'to have a ship with a chart house on the poop [the raised deck right aft where the officers kept their watches and the captain took exercise]. It will be so convenient to do my sewing in.' What the owner said later about his new Captain's wife—admittedly he had it from the ship's officers—was that she knew quite a lot about navigation and ship's business and assisted her husband considerably in the day-to-day work on board. She signed on the ship's Articles as purser at a shilling a month.

The *Wray Castle* loaded coals in September, 1917, at the Alexander Dock in Newport but did not leave until the 1st November, when she was towed to Barry Roads to await a naval escort. But none was available and she was towed to sea on the 3rd November. Although the weather was bad the tug did not cast off her tow rope until the 7th November, when it was blowing a westerly gale.

The ship arrived at Grytricken on the 2nd January, 1918. She had reached a position off the island in 57 days and had covered a distance of 7,082 nautical miles, but, owing to thick weather, Captain Frampton could not make port. When she arrived on the first occasion a whaler started to tow her in but the tow rope parted in a gale and it was another two days before a second whaler came out of port and succeeded in towing her in.

After discharging the coals the *Wray Castle* took in ballast and, on the 6th February, sailed to Melbourne in 48 days. The best day's run (24 hours) was 304 nautical miles. She arrived at Williamstown on the 26th March, 1918. Grain was loaded for New York, the ship sailing from Hobson's Bay on the 11th May. At this time the policy was to keep the sailing ships out of the European war zone and when the *Wray Castle* arrived at New York on the 12th September, 1918, there were a number of windjammers there. It will be remembered that this was the time of the epidemic of Spanish 'flu, and the *Wray Castle* was fortunate in not losing any of her crew serving on board. She left New York loaded on the 12th November, 1918, for Melbourne, making a passage of 90 days. Arriving there on the 10th February, 1919 she discharged her general cargo and, there being no grain on offer, she sailed for Newcastle on the 7th March. This short passage took a fortnight. The coals loaded there were consigned to Gatico in Chile.

Leaving Newcastle on the 24th April, she arrived at Gatico on the 2nd July, 1919. After unloading her cargo of coals she sailed up the coast on the 25th July, in ballast, for Caleta Buena, some 20 miles northward of Iquique. It was an easy passage, with the Humboldt Current and the south-east trade winds combining to give a three days' fair wind passage.

At Caleta Buena the *Wray Castle* loaded nitrate for Cape Town.

Although she had been owned by Sir William Garthwaite for about eighteen months her name and port of registry had not been altered. It was at Caleta Buena that a young man, John Prothero Williams, joined her as first mate, having been sent on the owners' orders, from the *Juteopolis*, which was then lying at anchor at Carrizal Bajo in Chile. He is now Captain Sir John Prothero Williams, CMG, OBE, Chairman of the Australian National Line of Steamships. He was created a Knight Bachelor in 1967 for his services to Australian shipping.

There can be no question that he was the most proficient and successful first mate serving in Sir William Garthwaite's fleet of windjammers. And this is no reflection on the others, many of whom were first-class. He was so outstanding that a brief record of his sea career and his work ashore must be included in this book. Captain Sir John Prothero Williams was born in Hull in 1896. His father came from Wales, his mother was English and his early years were spent at Carne in Carmarthen, South Wales. He was educated at Queen Elizabeth's Grammar School and served his sea apprenticeship in steamers. He wanted sail experience, so obtained it the hard way, by serving before the mast. After passing his square-rigged second mate's examination he served as second mate in the *Saint Mirren* and *Neotsfield*, both windjammers being sunk by enemy submarines in the first world war while he was serving in them.

His next windjammer was the *Juteopolis* which he joined at Bahia Blanca, Argentine, as second mate when Mr Garthwaite bought her in 1917.

While the *Wray Castle* had been discharging her cargo Mr Kelk, her first mate, was injured so badly that he was sent to hospital. Another first mate had to take his place, and, as the acting second mate did not hold a certificate, Mr Williams was sent from the *Juteopolis* on the 21st August, 1919, so that the ship could sail when the loading of her cargo was completed. Mr A O Zrinyi, a naturalised British subject, forty-six years of age, held a British second mate's square-rigged certificate and he was promoted to acting first mate of the *Juteopolis* at £25 a month. These changes were instructions from the owners. Mr Allen, the senior apprentice of the *Wray Castle* was acting as her second mate; Mr Williams described him as 'a first-class officer'.

Young Mr Williams had to make his own way north by railway to Iquique and then by steamer to Caleta Buena of which he said: 'the mountains [Andes] run almost vertically down to the sea and the town is perched on little bits of shelves here and there, some of it built on bags of nitrate'.

The seamen had all deserted the *Wray Castle* with the exception of two Scandinavians, and the new first mate's job was to go to Iquique and get a crew as the ship was almost loaded. Mr Williams was told of a 'hard-up' sailors' boarding house run by Mrs Brady and he went to see her. It was the usual West Coast of South America sailors' 'dump', bare with bunks two high in every room like a seaman's fo'c'sle. There were even bunks in the entrance passage. Half-drunk seamen were lolling about and young Williams had to push his way through them to find Mrs Brady. Her late husband, Jim Brady, had been a coloured fighter and crimp who had supplied ships' crews by shanghaing sailors on board ships when they were dead drunk. He had left the business to his wife. She was a Chilean woman whom Mr Williams described as 'a huge woman, six feet high and nearly three feet wide with a mane of black hair and a square, hard face'. She was obviously well able to take charge of the seamen she supplied and did so with success. He had a few drinks with her but was quite unable to match her drink for drink. He said: 'If I had done so I might have found myself on some ship outward bound.'

Mr Williams had to bargain with her for the price of each man to be 'shipped' on the *Wray Castle*. Fourteen were wanted and the usual agreement was made whereby she drew their advance note for a month's pay which was to be paid to her after the men had actually sailed in the ship. She also demanded 'blood money'; a hundred Chilian pesos for each man. The agreement was that she was to have them all on board in two days. These men would have been taking advantage of Mrs Brady's 'hospitality' in her Boarding House and would pay for their keep to her, perhaps a little more, by presenting her with a month's advanced pay. The 'Blood Money' would be supplied by the ship's owner in return for her services in supplying the men and delivering them on board the ship.

Two days later the sound of a boat's engine was heard approaching the

Wray Castle in the bay at Caleta Buena. Then terrific curses were heard from Mrs Brady as the boat came alongside the ship with a bump. All the seamen in the boat were drunk and the lady was endeavouring to get them up the rope ladder and on to the deck when the three mates came to give a hand. One of the new crew had received her 'persuasion' with more force than was necessary and was lying unconscious in the bottom of the boat. They were all helped along to the fo'c'sle and disposed of in the bunks. Mrs Brady then went aft with the mates to the small mess room used by the officers. Captain and Mrs Frampton had retired discreetly to their room, which young Mr Williams said was just as well. They gave Mrs Brady the whisky bottle, had a couple of drinks themselves, and then passed it back. She finished the remaining half bottle without turning a hair.

Sam Elfick, the third mate, who had given a hand with the drunken seamen, was a good-looking, stalwart young lad with beautiful golden hair and bright blue eyes. Mrs Brady took a fancy to him at once and it was all that Mr Williams and Mr Allen could do to keep her off him. They succeeded by giving the lady another bottle of whisky followed by a large pannikin of black coffee and away she went in her boat to Iquique. They wondered what kind of life Mr Brady must have had with her and agreed that his love-life must have been something.

The seamen that Mrs Brady had brought to the ship were a mixed bunch. Among them were Vajiski and Levine, Russian Jews, who, rumour had it, were said to have robbed a bank in Argentine and got away over the Andes; Kona, an excellent Japanese able seaman; three Peruvian soldiers; an Arab fireman and a couple of Scandinavians. The others were nondescript and out of the lot only the Scandinavians and the Japanese had ever served in a sailing ship before. But a little 'up aloft' practice was got in before the ship sailed, and, after sobering up, they soon got the hang of the positions of the braces, halliards, downhauls, buntlines and leechlines and the work on deck.

After the cargo was loaded, and the hatches on the holds were battened down, two days were spent in preparing for sea, the hours of working being the usual ones in port of from 6 am to 6 pm. One anchor was hove up and the other was hove short (to 30 or 45 fathoms) one afternoon and evening, and at dawn on the 8th September, 1919, when the cold air came down from the mountain top into the bay and gave an off-shore wind, the *Wray Castle*'s crew hove in the cable of the anchor still out, and gave her an off-shore slant by backing the sails on the foremast. She swung round and headed out to sea, and, with her yards trimmed to the fair wind, cleared the bay and set a course to the southward and Cape Horn whence the ship would sail across the South Atlantic to Cape Town.

The weather was kind and gave the new hands four days of fine weather in which to get used to the ship and settle down. Then followed a light to moderate gale which, although not giving them a true test, did give them an idea of what they would have to contend with off Cape Horn. They learned how to stand on the main deck and pull on the braces, when the ship was taking seas over, without flinching. They were a poor crowd when they came on board, starved and drink-sodden, but the good sea air, and even the 'pound and pint' fare of the windjammer, improved their health and physique considerably and by the time the ship got down to Cape Horn they were quite a good crew.

Cape Horn was rounded and the run across the South Atlantic was made with no damage to masts and spars or casualties to the crew. They made an excellent team and the mates hoped to keep them. Cape Town was reached on the 13th November, 1919, after a passage of 66 days. The flesh-pots of the shore pulled at them but they were prohibited immigrants and there was no danger of them attempting to desert the ship until her last week's stay in port when they hoped they could hide until the ship had sailed. One or two did make a break for it but they were picked up by the police and held until the ship was about to sail and then put on board.

After the nitrate had been discharged ballast was taken on board and the ship left on the 18th December, for Newcastle, New South Wales. It was on this passage that Captain Brinley Byrne, an apprentice and brother of the late Captain E G Byrne, who was third mate of the *Garthsnaid*, fell down the hold and broke the bones in both legs. His left thigh was fractured in two places and the right thigh in one place. Mr Williams and Mr Allen got him up out of the hold into the cabin aft and, in accordance with the 'Shipmaster's Medical Guide', put a cork in his mouth to prevent him biting his tongue while they were carrying out first aid. They laid him down on the saloon floor and the first mate put his foot into his crutch to help pull his legs into their right position. The second mate felt the fractures, to make sure the legs were back in their right place, and then pieces of timber were put down on each side of his legs, and lashed up with canvas. Mr Williams wrote to me telling me that all through this very painful job young Byrne remained conscious and never made a murmur. He was then put in the steward's bunk, off the saloon, and remained there for three weeks until the ship arrived in Newcastle on the 17th February, 1920, when he was taken ashore to hospital.

It was found that one leg was shorter than the other, the reason being that there were two fractures in the right leg and only one in the left. This gave him a limp but in spite of this, years later, he was the opening bat for the Swansea Cricket Club. Later still, in about 1932 when he was serving in Swansea tugs, the tow-rope of his tug parted, and, swinging round, hit his right leg, fracturing it again. When the leg was set it became the same length as the left one which had been broken in two places previously. He lost his limp, although he was about three inches shorter than he was before his legs were fractured.

There was a further sequel to this unlucky accident; a very happy one. Dr Grieves, the Hon Physician in Charge at the Newcastle Hospital, asked his daughter to take young Byrne some books and fruit. At the same time Mr Williams went to see Byrne and met Miss Grieves. Captain Sir John Williams wrote to the author: 'She later became my wife. Before that I had no intention whatsoever of settling in Australia. Strange, is it not, what things decide one's fate. The fact that Byrne broke his leg led me to this country [Australia] which has showered so many blessings on my head since I came to settle here so many, many years ago now.'

How successful he has been has already been related, but I am sure it will be agreed that it was his outstanding ability and business acumen that has got him where he is today. Even so the author is just as sure that his training in the windjammers has been of great help to him.

The officers of the sailing ships which Captain Frampton commanded did not always get on well with him. Captain Sir John Williams suggests that in his case it was his own fault. I do not think so. Any captain who draws attention to his officers' shortcomings, real or imaginary, in front of the crew makes it difficult for the officer to keep discipline on board.

Captain Frampton had a habit of coming on deck in fine weather and wanting the yards trimmed with more exactitude. There was nothing wrong with this; but the way he was said to go about it was certainly open to criticism. Captain Sir John Williams explained Captain Frampton's method. He would stand at the break of the poop when the first or second mate was slacking away the braces and shout out: 'A little bit more on the lower', or 'check in the upper a bit more'. It was more than young Williams could stand; especially as he had had some years of experience of the practical side of trimming yards—certainly more than Captain Frampton had had. So the first time this happened to him he made the braces fast, went up on the poop to the Captain, and told him politely that if he wanted to trim the yards then he should go down on the deck and do so and he (young Williams) would go to his cabin. Captain Frampton took it very well and there was no trouble at all between him and his first mate after that. But in spite of this it must be said that Captain Frampton was an excellent windjammer master; more, he was one of the best.

Mrs Frampton had the reputation of being extremely knowledgeable on the work in sailing ships, and, considering she had sailed with her husband most, if not all, of their married life, this is not surprising. Young Williams fell foul of her soon after sailing from Caleta Buena. It was when that gale they met four days after leaving was approaching. He was not surprised. He had been warned. She came up on the poop and told him to take the main topgallant sail in. He told her he took orders only from the Captain and after that the relationship between them was strained for the whole of the remainder of the voyage.

In most windjammers the mates, and especially the apprentices, found the captains' wives helpful, often making life on board much easier for them. But Captain Joseph Conrad, the sea-writer, found that this was not so on the outward-bound passage of the ship *Riversdale* which he made as second mate in 1883–1884. He left the ship in Madras after a dispute with his captain which may have been caused by an interference of the captain's wife. Conrad referred to this in his novel *Chance* where the ship is given the name *Ferndale*. Here, the second mate joining the ship in London finds that the captain is taking his wife on the voyage and remarks that he has heard that captains' wives can cause a lot of trouble on board if they take a dislike to anyone: especially if they were new wives who were young and pretty. Conrad also wrote that the older ones, who had made many voyages, imagined that they knew more about handling the ship than their husbands and 'had an eye like a hawk for what went on'. He continued: 'In the general opinion a skipper with his wife on board was more difficult to please; but whether to show off his authority before an admiring female, or from living anxiety for her safety, or simply from irritation at her presence, nobody I ever heard on the subject could tell for certain.' Women don't change!

Mrs Frampton was a seasoned sailor. Her elder daughter was born at sea and the younger one was only three weeks old when she started her first voyage. The girls were brought up in windjammers, and they were the only homes Mrs Frampton knew since she joined the *Ballumbie* in 1901. Both daughters made voyages in the windjammers of Sir William Garthwaite.

The *Wray Castle* discharged her ballast at Stockton in an unusual way, which I had not heard of in that port. Nothing seems more unlikely than a horse hoisting the baskets of ballast out of the hold; yet this did in fact happen. The horse pulled on a rope attached to him by a bridle, and walked along the deck pulling the rope through lead blocks until the loaded basket was above the level of the hatch, when it was swung to the ship's side and emptied into a barge below. The horse knew exactly how far he had to walk and no ordering or coaxing would get him to walk another pace. Mr Williams called him a 'Union' horse. He would not start work until eight bells had been rung in the morning at 8 am, and would not work after eight bells had been struck at noon. And in the afternoon he knew that two bells, 1 pm, was the time for starting and two bells at 5 pm was the time for knocking off for the day. He always answered to his name 'Chess', which was probably given to him because he was chestnut-coloured. Everybody on board was very fond of him.

Mr Allen, the second mate, finished his apprenticeship in Newcastle and paid off the ship there, and Mr A G Spiers joined her in his place. Mr Williams thought a lot of him as a seaman and watchkeeping officer. He had had a great deal of experience in sailing ships, having served in the *British Yeoman*, the *Lord Templeton* and many others including the four-masted barques of Andrew Weir's Bank Line.

One thing that upset Mr Williams at the end of the ship's stay in Newcastle was something that happened far too often in windjammers. The *Wray Castle*, after finishing loading her coals, was towed out to the Farewell Buoy at the mouth of the river on Friday evening, and Captain Frampton said that she would stay there until Monday morning. Mr Williams made arrangements to accompany his future wife and her parents on a picnic that Saturday afternoon, but at noon a tug brought Captain and Mrs Frampton back to the ship, and it was announced that the ship would sail immediately. Young Williams' future wife's house overlooked the entrance to the river and he saw her standing on the verandah in a white frock waving a big hat, knowing it could be twelve months before they met again. To me this seemed very ungrateful considering that Mr Williams had looked after the ship in Cape Town while the Captain and his wife went up country for a holiday, and the ship had also been left to the first mate to look after while she was in Newcastle. Very much too much was left to the young first mates in windjammers in port.

The *Wray Castle* had loaded her coals for Iquique in Chile. While in Newcastle the two mates had made a thorough overhaul of the gear of the sails hoping to make a really good passage across the South Pacific. The ship sailed on the 15th March, 1920, and arrived at Iquique on the 6th May, being 52 days on the passage. It was pleasant and uneventful with fine weather most of the way but not exactly a fast passage. George Spiers, the new second mate, had fought boxing matches in the ring and was a good boxer. He had a few rounds with Mr Williams and the apprentices on deck and taught them a lot about aggression and self-defence. The crew watched the bouts with interest and there was no trouble with them after that.

There was a method used on the *Wray Castle* which gave a greater out-turn of coal in Iquique than was loaded in Newcastle. Although guilty of participating in the practice, I had never heard of this particular method. The baskets used for hauling the coal out of the holds were dried out thoroughly in the heat of the galley before the ship arrived at Iquique. Then they were weighed in the presence of the Chilean tally clerk on arrival. This was done to get the weight of the coal in the basket, the weight of the basket being subtracted from the weight of the coal and basket as recorded on the scale. Then, before work started each morning, the baskets were well soaked in water, adding considerably to their weight and the weight of the combined basket and coal. This meant that the difference of the weight of the wet and dry baskets was added on to the tallied weight of coal that was discharged into the barge. It all sounds rather elementary and easy of detection but the Chilean tally clerk was usually in the racket and got his rake-off. It was indeed difficult to make the British windjammers pay in the last years of their existence.

Iquique, as we know, had its temptations ashore and Mr Williams warned the apprentices against the brothels and their inhabitants. He told them a story concerning an apprentice serving in another ship anchored in Iquique some years before. He knew the first mate of the ship personally, and he told the story as a warning to the lads in the *Wray Castle*. It is not without interest and shows the extraordinary outlook on life of the prostitutes in those brothels.

This first mate warned the lads in his ship of the dangers of visiting these places of ill repute and they were quite indignant that he thought they might even consider it. They drew their money and went ashore for their day's holiday, which was known as 'Liberty Day'. Several days later one of the indignant youths came repentantly to the mate and told him that he thought he was suffering from a disease contracted from a prostitute. It was seen that he was, and the mate took him to the captain so that arrangements could be made for the lad to have medical treatment ashore. The captain was one of those sanctimonious 'holier than thou' type of shipmasters who were sometimes found in windjammers, and he dismissed the whole thing with: 'If he has sinned he should suffer!' He would do nothing to help the lad.

The mate studied the 'Shipmaster's Medical Guide' but could find nothing in the Medicine Chest on board which would help, so he determined that he would take the lad ashore early next morning. That night the youngster was so worried that he determined to end it all and jumped overboard into the Bay. The mate had warned the other apprentices to keep a watch on him, but it was the third mate who jumped in after him, and with the help of his shipmates, got him out. They stayed with him all night until the morning when the mate took him ashore. He was taken to the British Consul, who got him into the local hospital immediately and sent with him for his treatment a supply of salvarsan, which was hardly known out there at that time. He recovered in a matter of weeks.

There was a sequel to this. On Sunday mornings it was the custom of the women from the brothels to attend Mass and then go hospital-visiting. The mate happened to be paying a visit to the lad when the 'ladies of the town' arrived. Three of them were sitting on the lad's bed trying to make conversation with him. One was quite young, and, with that kind sympathy so admirable in the tender sex, pressed him to join her in the next cubicle, which was empty. She did not disguise her intentions so the lad pulled up the sleeve of his pyjama coat, showed the 'lady' the scars of his injections and said in pigeon English 'No possiblee, plenty pox!' With a gay laugh she pulled up her sleeve and showing her scars said 'No importa! lo mismo!' (That's nothing! I'm the same!) : So lightly was the disease regarded in these coast ports at that time. Happily the young fellow made a complete recovery and rejoined his ship before she sailed. Not only was he much wiser; so were his shipmates.

Some of the crew of the *Wray Castle* deserted the ship in Iquique and as Mrs Brady had apparently retired, other means had to be adopted to replace them. A French four-masted barque was lying at anchor near to the *Wray Castle* and, hearing that her officers were all ashore, Mr Williams and the second mate boarded her late one afternoon. They talked to the men in the fo'c'sle and told them of the high wages paid in British ships, the good food supplied and the kind treatment accorded to the seamen; then they advanced the fact that there were some vacancies in the *Wray Castle*. Five French seamen were interested, and so, after dark, with a few bottles of extra-good wine, the two officers went back to the French barque and invited them over for a meal. They put on a special feast to impress the French sailors. There was plenty to drink and no trouble at all in persuading them to 'jump' their ship and sail in the *Wray Castle*.

There were still a couple of hands short, and when the two mates heard of an American steamer whose captain had a man he wanted to get rid of they paid a visit to him. The captain called him 'a real booze artist and troublemaker'. They thought that he would indeed be a 'booze artist' if he got hold of any in the *Wray Castle;* it was all carefully locked away under Captain Frampton's eye aft. So the two mates boarded the American steamer at midnight, when the man was partly drunk, and gave him an invitation to a party with girls, that was being held on their ship. Having got him on board their ship they gave him a few more drinks, and then made him up a rough bed in the fore peak where he stayed until he sobered up, by which time the ship had sailed.

It is the author's intention to record, as far as he knows, the type of men who served in the last of the British windjammers, and George Spiers, the second mate of the *Wray Castle* at this time, certainly deserves mentioning. When he joined the ship at Newcastle, New South Wales, it was his resolve to get to London to visit his old home and his sisters. His present home was then in Newcastle, New South Wales, where he had a wife and four children. He assigned the whole of his pay to his wife and intended to work his way back to Australia from London. All he had with him was a ten-shilling note which he insisted would get him a couple of meals and would tide him over until he got some employment.

When, at Iquique, he learned that the *Wray Castle* was loading for Lourenço Marques, East Africa, he asked to be paid off from her. Captain Frampton agreed and Mr Spiers joined an American steamer where he was offered a job as a passage worker to New Orleans. He found that his job was to be an unpaid second mate. When the steamer arrived at New Orleans he left her and got accommodation with the Salvation Army for a few days and then he heard that the British steamer *Gascoyne*, in Newport News, wanted a crew. He got there by jumping trains or hitch-hiking on motor trucks and signed on her as an able seaman. He paid off at a French port and made for London with his small amount of pay. Mr Williams then carries on with the story:

> A year or more went by and I arrived out in Australia first mate of a steamer, having by then obtained my master's certificate. I had brought all my study books with me. While serving on the Australian coast I met George Spiers in Adelaide. Times were hard. He had five children by then and the only employment offered was as a sail-maker in Russell's sail loft in that port. George wanted to get back to sea again, but, having no certificate, felt that if he started again in the fo'c'sle on the Australian coast he'd never get out of it. And it was hard enough getting an able seaman's job there at that time.
>
> I suggested to George that I'd give him my study books and he should have a shot at getting a second mate's certificate. He agreed that he'd have a try but reckoned it was hopeless as he hadn't the time or the money to go to a school. But he took the books and two months later I got a telegram to say he had passed for his certificate. He used to knock off work at five o'clock, go home and have his tea, and go to bed setting the alarm clock to wake him up at two in the morning when he'd study till breakfast time, after which he'd go to work. Week-ends he'd study all day and half the night.
>
> An even more startling performance followed. George got a job as second mate on a coaster out of Adelaide, and the next thing I knew was that he'd passed for first mate, then master, and later succeeded in getting his extra master's certificate. He was promoted to master and eventually was appointed a pilot in Adelaide. And there, now retired, he lives and we meet from time to time and brace the yards round again in the *Wray Castle* of long ago.

Captain Spiers piloted Captain Erikson's Finnish windjammers in and out of the South Australian grain ports without tugs in the St Vincent and Spencer Gulfs on many occasions. Captain Sir J P Williams thinks it very likely that he was the last man in the world to sail a big windjammer alongside a pier and later sail her away without tugs.

After George Spiers left the *Wray Castle* one of the able seamen was appointed second mate. Although a good seaman Mr Williams concluded that he was not as good an officer as George Spiers.

Captain Frampton knew that the ship was shorthanded before leaving Iquique and had said to Mr Williams, 'I suppose you will get the men somewhere!' So when the Frenchmen and the American were brought aft to the saloon to sign on the ship's 'Articles of Agreement' he did not inquire where they came from. The French sailors were all Bretons, probably the best type of seamen that France has produced. Mr Williams described them as: 'ruddy-faced, chunky, short men and splendid seamen, every one'. He continued:

> I believe they liked the ship and certainly I liked them and was thankful to have them on board. I recollect they brought a number of 'penny dreadfuls' with them, printed in French, of course. I borrowed them and spent the passage, to my pleasure, learning French again, and, by practising when one of the French seamen was at the wheel in fine weather, I became able to speak it reasonably well by the time we got to Lourenço Marques.

When the ship sailed at dawn from Iquique the off-mountain breeze was light and fitful, and, as she neared the 'Point' at the entrance to the Bay, it failed and the ship was almost caught aback. Captain Frampton, aft on the poop, saw in the distance the ripple on the surface of the sea which gave warning of the change of direction of the wind. It was his prompt orders to brace the fore yards round that enabled the ship to be backed away from the shore and so prevented her from being driven on to the rocks. She cleared the Bay braced sharp up on the port tack.

The passage to Lourenço Marques was mostly a fine weather one. As the ship was approaching the pilot boat on arriving off Lourenço Marques, the wind went round suddenly and blew from ahead. The mainsail was hauled up and with an excellent crew, the ship was promptly tacked. She came round under full sail in a fresh breeze. Before the pilot could be picked up, a second tack had to be made which brought the ship round just as successfully as the first. As she approached the pilot boat, her crew cheered the officers and crew of the *Wray Castle* for their fine seamanship as displayed by their perfect tacking of their ship. Here is what Captain Sir J P Williams remembers of that arrival:

> A bright sparkling morning with the breeze raising white caps on the top of the seas all round. The entrance to the harbour just discernible. The ship ready to go about [tack]. 'Keep her clean full!' to the man at the wheel, and she's run off a bit. 'Hard a lee!' and down goes the wheel and she comes up into the wind. A minute, perhaps, watching her closely and then 'Mainsail Haul!' and the main yards are hauled round to the sound of the rattling of the patent sheaves in the blocks. Then the sails on the main began to fill and the order came from aft: 'Fore Bowline!' By this time the men are standing by the fore braces and in a few minutes the yards are round and the ship's braced sharp up on the other tack. With all the sails full save for the ripple of the clews of the royals. And the ship is quiet again and the men are coiling down the ropes. And now [1967] I, and those like me, the tattered remnant of a vanished age, are thankful in our hearts to have been part of that life.

This was Captain Sir J P Williams' last passage in the old windjammers. He wrote that this part of his life gave him more satisfaction than anything else with the exception of his salvage successes which came later. He also had something to say about the American sailor, who had been taken on board the ship at Iquique, and was left in a drunken condition in the fore peak just before the ship sailed. After he sobered up he soon got the hang of sailing ship work and became an excellent windjammer seaman. While he was in the ship in Lourenço Marques he gave no sign of taking strong drink; in fact he was a thoroughly sober and good living man. What was more difficult to understand was that he never inquired how he got down in the fore peak of the *Wray Castle*. Had the life in the windjammer given him a different outlook on life?

Mr Williams signed off the Ship's Articles with the rest of the crew of the *Wray Castle* at the end of that voyage at Lourenço Marques on the 20th October, 1920, and went home to pass his examination for master, square-rigged, or, as it was called in those days, the Ordinary Certificate as opposed to the Steamship Certificate.

Later he served in ships owned in Australia and then took up wharf management, stevedoring and marine salvage in Australia with great success. His most successful salvage operation was the recovery of gold valued at £2,379,000 from the RMS *Niagra*, owned by the Canadian Australasian Line, which had been sunk in 420 feet of water in Hauriki Gulf off the east coast of North Island, New Zealand, on the 19th June, 1940.

The *Garthwray*: the longest passage ever

In October 1920, while in Lourenço Marques, Captain Frampton was informed of the change of the name of his ship from *Wray Castle* to *Garthwray*. New Articles of Agreement for the signing on of the new crew were opened on the 27th October, 1920, and in them the registered port of the ship was recorded as Liverpool and the name and address of her owners were given as: The Marine Navigation Company Limited, 92/94 Gracechurch Street, London EC. The Agreement was for:

> A voyage not exceeding three years' duration to any ports or places within the limits of latitudes 75° north and 60° south, commencing at Lourenço Marques, proceeding thence to Australia or any other ports within the above limits, trading in any rotation, and to end at such port in the United Kingdom or Continent of Europe (within Home Trade limits) as may be required by the master
>
> The seamen shall mutually assist each other in the general duties of the ship.
>
> The crew shall be deemed to be complete with 14 hands all told of whom not less than eight shall be sailors.

There were three apprentices serving on board and the crew members, including the apprentices but excluding the two mates and the captain, numbered seventeen, so there would be nine hands in the fo'c'sle. The able seamen signed on at £12 a month.

Captain Frampton was then 63 years of age. The new first mate, Mr F G Campbell, was 49 and received £25 a month and Mr William Hayes from Guernsey, also 49 years of age, was signed on as bosun and acted as second mate. D Sinclair from Stromness, aged 34, signed on as able seaman and was promoted to acting second mate when William Hayes left in Sydney.

Miss Eva Frampton, the daughter of Captain and Mrs Frampton, came out from home to join the ship and her parents at Lourenço Marques, signing on as flag-maker at a shilling a month. She was then eighteen years of age. It will be remembered that she had sailed with her parents in windjammers before the First World War. She had left school to join the ship, her father having promised her one more voyage in a sailing ship to complete her education.

The *Garthwray* left Lourenço Marques on the 19th December, 1920, in ballast for Sydney, Australia. When she arrived on the 7th February, 1921, there was no cargo for her to load so she was towed north to Newcastle, on the 19th February, to load coals for Valparaiso, Chile.

Miss Frampton had found life at school dull after her early years at sea. She was fascinated with life on board when the ship was out at sea and not at all interested in visiting ports. She took great interest in the fish and birds and was always excited at the prospect of collecting Gulf Weed in the Sargasso Sea. Bad weather conditions had never worried her. 'Daddy was captain so there was no danger!' So when she joined the *Garthwray* she looked forward to the voyage and the life at sea. She liked watching the work of trimming the yards, tacking or wearing ship, making fast and setting sail. She had the biggest thrill of all when she was allowed to take a trick at the wheel and steer the ship. She felt she had the ship completely under her control. She liked steering at night for she could then get a star in line with the leech of one of the square sails, and when the ship sheered away from the star she could, by turning the wheel a few spokes, arrest her movement and bring her back on course. This movement of the ship's head was seen so much more quickly with the help of a star than with the compass. The moon shining on the white canvas sails, the glittering of the stars in the velvet sky, and the white tops on the dark sea always gave her a thrill like nothing she experienced ashore.

She carried out her duties as flag-maker although they were chiefly concerned with repairing the flags. Eva and her mother did a great deal of needlework and they had a good library on board. Captain Frampton bought his daughter a piano at Lourenço Marques so they were never short of music at sea. She and her mother took charge of the slop chest, the ship's shop, and sold the mates, apprentices and crew tobacco, cigarettes, clothes, blankets, oilskins and seaboots etc. every Saturday evening in the second dog-watch, from 6 pm to 8 pm. The goods were spread out on the saloon table. Everything bought was booked up against the purchaser, and at the end of the voyage was totalled and deducted from his wages. Masters of the old windjammers were reputed to have bought rows of houses from the profits made, but, although they did get some return for providing a necessary and beneficial service, the profits were never on the get-rich-quick scale suggested. It was an especial boon to those seamen who came on board to start the voyage destitute and with only the clothes they had on; and there were many of those in windjammer days. Imagine what life would have been for them, down in the gales of the Roaring Forties, wet through from the icy seas smashing on board because they had no oilskins and seaboots, or cold because they had no blankets on their bunks (for these were not supplied by the owners), to say nothing of life without tobacco for the smokers. The slop chest was invaluable in the windjammers.

Chickens were kept on the *Garthwray* for their eggs; there was also a pig which, although kept on board for fresh food became, as on all ships, a much-loved pet. All ship's pigs were given the name of Dennis and although their home was a spacious pen in the protection of the fore side of the deck house on the fore deck, in fine weather they had the freedom of the whole of the main deck where they were made a fuss of by members of the crew. Dennis on the *Garthwray* often went into the saloon aft to pay a visit to Mrs Frampton and Eva. Pigeons were also kept on board the *Garthwray* as pets and were free to fly out to sea and round the ship in the daytime, always returning to their loft on board for the night.

Eva Frampton mixed freely with the officers and apprentices aft, but rarely went forward of the mainmast. She often helped the apprentices with their studies for their second mate's examinations. One onerous task was learning by heart the thirty-one, afterwards thirty-two, articles for The Prevention of Collisions at Sea. They had to be repeated, parrot-fashion, in the examination room. Eva listened patiently to the lads struggling through them, correcting them when necessary. She also helped with the mathematics of the navigation problems.

The *Garthwray* left Newcastle on the 17th May, 1921, for Valparaiso, Chile, and arrived there on the 17th July. While the coal was being discharged a warning of a 'Norther' was given. Northers blew into the Bay from the north with the force of a hurricane, set up a dangerous sea, and, on occasions, carried away the ship's anchor cables and drove the ships ashore with the loss of the ships and many of their crews.

While the *Garthwray* was moored in Valparaiso Bay a Norther struck the ships there. She was moored at the buoys. When the warning was given the Frampton family were ashore. The ship's agent tried to persuade them against returning to the ship, but naturally, Captain Frampton insisted that he must be on board when the 'Norther' struck her, and his wife and daughter insisted on going with him. The weather had become rough already and big seas were running into the Bay and swamping the launch in which they were going back to the ship. The steamers had all hove-up their anchors and steamed out to sea for safety. Extra moorings were put out on the buoys and the *Garthwray* rode safely through that terrible night.

Not long before the ship arrived at Valparaiso the Rev T Hardy, of The Missions to Seamen, was ordained by the Bishop of South America and the Falklands and remained there as chaplain. His was the first Anglican ordination that had ever taken place in the port. He held his first Communion Service on board the *Garthwray*. Mr Hardy had joined The Missions to Seamen as a lay reader on the 12th January, 1904, and was appointed to the Valparaiso 'Mission' in 1906. The Rev the Hon C Cumming Bruce went to the port to investigate the possibilities of starting work in the ports on the West Coast of South America and this resulted in Mr Hardy's appointment. There was no Institute ashore then and his work consisted of ship-visiting and holding Church Services on the Pacific Steam Navigation Company's hulk *Lontué*.

In 1907 an Institute was opened and the Rev A R Harper-Smith became chaplain with Mr Hardy as his lay-reader. The launch *Victory* was dedicated on the 6th February, 1910, to assist in the work with the ships in the Bay, and, later that year, the Rev Harper-Smith left the port. After his ordination in 1920, the Rev T Hardy became Chaplain. He was instrumental in designing, and he opened, a new Institute in Valparaiso on the 24th May, 1926.

Mr F G Campbell, the first mate, was paid off at Valparaiso and his place was taken by Mr J M McLeod, aged 53, who was born at Inverness in Scotland but gave his home address as Copiapo, Chile. He signed on on the 5th September, 1921, at £25 a month.

The *Garthwray* left Valparaiso early in September and sailed in ballast for Taltal arriving there on the 26th September, 1921. She loaded nitrate for Falmouth for orders, leaving on the 22nd October. On the passage home fine weather was enjoyed. Cape Horn was rounded at ten knots, with all sail set, in wonderfully good weather in a blue sea with fine-weather cirrus clouds in the sky. It was, of course, mid-summer. Cape Horn was sighted with the sun shining on the ice on the mountain top.

A good passage of 83 days was made to Falmouth where orders were received to proceed to Leith to discharge the cargo. Here came the worst part of the passage. It took 30 days to sail round to Leith in the worst weather possible. Besides strong gales, which caused the ship to be hove-to under lower topsails, head winds were also met. The *Garthwray* started to leak badly, and, when the crew were not bracing the yards or handling the sails, they had to man the pumps. The worst weather was met in the North Sea and when the gales eased the ship had been driven 140 miles to the northward of the Firth of Forth, and Captain Frampton put into Cromarty. A big salvage tug towed her back to Leith. She arrived at Leith on the 16th February after having been away from the United Kingdom since the 1st November, 1917, a period of four years, three months and fifteen days. Here Captain Frampton left left her and retired from the sea. His first command had been in the sailing ship *Earl's Court* in 1881, which gave him forty years in command of square-rigged sailing ships including the last of the windjammers. This must have been one of the longest periods as captain and his was certainly one of, if not *the* most successful careers in sailing ships.

Captain Edward Mann, then aged 54, relieved Captain Frampton. It will be remembered that he was master of the *Invercauld*, one of Sir William Garthwaite's early barques, when she was torpedoed and sunk in February, 1917. His next command had been the four-masted barque *Bellands*, and he came from her to the *Garthwray*. Mr J M McLeod continued in the ship as first mate although his wages were reduced to £19.10s a month, and Mr Duncan T Robertson, aged 47, from Saltcoats, Scotland, signed on as second mate at £15 a month. He had a second mate's certificate which was unusual for a windjammer second mate at that time. Ten able seamen signed on at £10 a month. There were also a sailmaker, carpenter, and cook-steward, besides the apprentices. The latter were; Daniel Watson Gray of Cape Town, Edward Victor Hayward of Bunbury, Western Australia, Frederick Vincent Simpson from Cue, Western Australia, Wilfred Robert Hobden of Cooma, New South Wales, Gerald H G Dunne of London, who was born at Edenderry, Ireland, Thomas Gray Valentine Ward of Hull, Lionel Adams of Brighton, now of Melbourne, Australia, George Alexander Kent of Liverpool and Leslie William Rolfe of Maidstone; nine apprentices who were excellent seamen, as were the able seamen. It was a good crew for a windjammer of this size, good in quality as well as numbers.

The *Garthwray* had been towed across the Firth of Forth to Grangemouth to load 3,000 tons of briquettes for Iquique. When she left on the 22nd July, 1922, a course was set round the north of Scotland. This avoided the long and tiring passage down the North Sea and through the English Channel, but even so Captain Mann was criticised by his crew for ordering the lighter sails to be furled late in the evening and having them set again in the early morning. They were sure that this made unnecessary work.

A long, fine weather passage was made to Cape Horn, the ship experiencing light, variable winds down to the Canary Islands. The north-east trade winds were also light and disappointing. But there were warm days and cool nights when the crew and apprentices could sleep in their bunks for the whole of their watch below—for at least three and a half hours—without the fear of that dreaded call: 'All hands on deck!' Even the watch on duty, on deck, could sometimes stretch out on one of the hatches for a short nap when they hadn't a trick at the wheel, a look-out on the fo'c'sle head, or time-keeping (striking the bell every half hour) on the poop.

It took a long time to work the ship through the doldrums with its calm, variable winds and torrential rains. Even the south-east trade winds, which were picked up a little north of the equator, were not as strong as usual. The crew did not look forward to the fight round the notorious Cape Horn against the westerly gales; but the passage had taken too long and the sooner they were down there the better. What they didn't know then was that they were to have far more than their fair share of it in the ensuing months.

They had a feeling of apprehension when they thought of Drake's Passage, that stretch of water to the southward of Cape Horn, where the worst weather and the steepest seas in the world are met. Heightened by continuous westerly gales, the seas sweeping round the world with no land to intercept them sometimes reach a height of from seventy to eighty feet. Seamen call them 'greybeards'. Great hills of water, capped with white surf, hurled themselves at the sailing ships passing that way. The unprotected wheels of windjammers were right aft and no helmsman was allowed to look over his shoulder up at one of those seas overtaking the ship. He might lose his nerve and run forward. A ship without a helmsman would broach-to and swing round into the trough of the sea. It would probably be the means of her capsizing, her loss and the loss of her crew.

It has been said that the winds off Cape Horn hardly ever blow at less than 45 miles per hour for twenty-two days in a month; and for five out of every seven of those days they blow from the westward. There does not appear to be any regular records kept of the losses of windjammers rounding Cape Horn, but between 1900 and 1914, fifty-three foundered, mostly with all hands.

'Rounding the Horn' was sailing from latitude 50° south in the South Atlantic Ocean to 50° south in the South Pacific, or vice-versa. Cape Horn is in latitude 55° 59′ south, longitude 67° 16′ west. Windjammer masters, when sailing from east to west, made 80° west before turning north into the Pacific Ocean. This was to make sure of not being set to leeward on to Chiloe Island, and the dangerous reefs off the western entrance to the Magellan Strait, where many windjammers have left their 'bones' after being stranded.

As far as I have been able to find out, the longest time taken to round Cape Horn in a westerly direction is 92 days by the French three-masted barque *Cambronne*; but masters of many windjammers gave up trying to get round, squared their yards, and sailed with a fair westerly wind right round the world to reach their ports in Chile. The quickest time ever made to the westward was six days in 1938 by the German four-masted barque *Priwall*.

June and July, mid-winter, are the best months to make a westerly rounding of the 'Horn' as the wind then sometimes blows from the eastward. It is all very much a matter of luck. In August and September strong westerly gales usually blow, and in the following two months the wind blows almost continually from the west.

When the *Garthwray* reached a position to the eastward of the Falkland Islands in the South Atlantic she experienced the start of bad weather. It became very cold, the wind increased to storm force and the seas were recorded as 'mountainous'. Sail was reduced to the three lower topsails and the storm staysails. When the wind eased to gale force the upper topsails were set, and, heeling over to the westerly gale-force wind, with water lapping into the lee scuppers, the *Garthwray* approached the latitude of Staten Island.

The wind was a dead-muzzler for rounding Cape Horn, and a strong east-setting current added to the difficulty. There was only one thing to do which might help to give them the westing which was imperative if they were to be successful; sail to the southward on the starboard tack until the wind shifted to the south of west and then put the ship round on the port tack and steer to the north-west. Ships rarely went further south than latitude 60°, the limit set by the Board of Trade, and, if there was no shift of wind, they would come north again to sight Cape Horn or Staten Island. The ship was then put round on the starboard tack and the run to the southward started once again. This procedure was often carried on for six weeks before a change of wind would give the ship a chance of making westing.

'Make westing at all costs!' was the maxim. With the yards braced sharp up and their sails kept just full (of wind) to prevent the ship making excessive leeway, their captains carried as much sail as they dared, making every mile to windward that was possible. It was known as 'head reaching' and the helm order was 'full and by', freely interpreted as 'by the wind with full sails'. In gales the windjammers could only be put round from one tack to another by 'wearing ship', that is going round before the wind.

This meant a loss of westing as compared with tacking, which is turning into the wind.

There were no easterly, or even southerly winds, for the *Garthwray*. She headed down towards the Antarctic, her crew keeping a good look out for ice. The cold seas swept over the starboard bulwarks and when the crew made their way along the main deck they could only do so with the help of the life lines. The deck houses, where the crew and the apprentices lived, were flooded; the lower bunks were soaked. No one had a dry stitch of clothing; oilskins were reduced to the texture of sodden brown paper. There was, of course, no means of heating the deck houses, and, when the galley fire was washed out, no immediate hope of hot food or even a hot drink. It was sheer misery. How long would it last?

The *Garthwray* was carrying her lower and upper topsails on her three masts as well as the big foresail and the fore and main topmast staysails. She made a brave show as her two helmsmen kept her as close to the wind as possible, keeping her sails full with a mere suspicion of a quiver in the weather clews of the upper topsails. 'Full and by' was their order, and they knew that every man who took his trick at the wheel helped or hindered the ship from making the vital westing. The hawk-like eyes of the officer in charge watched the sails and the compass; the Captain rarely left the poop.

They were reasonably lucky, for the wind was blowing from north of west, and the ship was making a course of about south-west. The easterly set of the current, and the leeway made by the ship, had to be reckoned with. When the *Garthwray* got down towards 60° south, the wind shifted to the southward, the crew wore her round on to the port tack, and she started to make the longed-for westing.

The sea now was not nearly so strong. The more sail that could be carried and the more speed gained meant a reduction of leeway.

Could it be that they were in luck at last? Were they going to make a really good time round Cape Horn? It certainly looked like it, for the gales lessened in force and Captain Mann decided to set the fore and main topgallant sails. The rolling eased, and, heeling over like a China clipper, she literally raced across the now subdued greybeards.

They had carried on like this all night and the crew could see no reason why they should not keep those topgallant sails on her all day. They were the big single type and what a difference they made to the ship's speed!

The crew decided it was all over except the shouting. And so it was; but not the way they thought. Captain Mann had come up on the poop at six o'clock that morning, given one look to windward, and ordered the officer of the watch to take in the two topgallant sails. It was obvious that the barometer had fallen for no apparent change in the weather could be discerned by the watch on deck. With that order went all hope of clearing the 'Horn' on that tack.

The yards were lowered in turn and the watch snugged the sails up to them. Then the order came: 'Up aloft and make them fast!' They divided in the usual way; apprentices and able seamen to each yard, and spread out along the footropes. The first folds of canvas were being held between them and the yard when a terrific squall hit the ship beam on. Over she went until the top of the lee bulwarks was under water. The canvas of the sails was ripped out from under their stomachs; they grabbed the backstays on top of the yards to save themselves from sliding down the footropes. Mercifully no one was thrown off into the sea or down to the deck below.

The yards were sloping at an angle of about forty degrees. They waited to hear the rumbling of the cargo shifting to the low side of the hold. Instead they heard the crack of the canvas of the upper topsails as it was rent with the force of the wind. That saved the ship. With the easing of side pressure she returned slowly to the upright. It seemed only a little; but it was enough to tell them that for a moment, at least, they were out of danger.

'All hands on deck!' The watch below were out almost before the order had blown away on the wind. Oilskins and seaboots had been dragged over their clothes and they grabbed their lengths of rope yarns which served as 'soul and body lashings' and tied them tightly round the bottom of their trousers, their waists and sleeves.

Up on the topgallant yards the watch on deck had started to make fast the sails again. But now the bellies of the canvas, held between the buntlines, were as hard as pumped-up tyres, and it became difficult to get the wind out of them, to get a handhold of canvas, to pull the skin of the belly towards them and hold it between the yards and their stomachs. Working together, as a team, they succeeded, each stretch of canvas gained making it easier every time.

They could hear the other watch down on deck hauling up the buntlines of the upper topsails. Their ship righted a little more.

Their fight with the topgallant sails over, they started to go down the rigging and met their shipmates coming up. They joined them on the upper topsail yards, and fought those flapping, banging sails together.

Before they got on deck again the hurricane-force squall had blown itself out. It had lasted for two hours. The decks were cleared, the ropes coiled up, and then a survey of the damage was made. The fore topgallant mast was sprung and split and the main topgallant mast split and fractured. It was a mercy that the masts had not come down when the men were aloft on the yards. The masts were secured. It was no longer possible to set any sails above the upper topsails on the fore or main masts. But that was not all. There was trouble with the wheel right aft on the poop, and it was found that rudder and rudder post were damaged; it was only by using a tackle on one side of the tiller that the ship could be steered. The fo'c'sle head, the main deck and the deck houses were also damaged with the heavy seas that crashed aboard in the squall. The wooden cover on the steering gear had blown away. This happened on the 11th November, 1922, when it was reported that the wind force recorded at the entrance to the Magellan Strait was 120 miles an hour. The night before the phenomenon of two identical moons, about fifteen degrees apart, had been seen from the *Garthwray*. Windjammer sailors believed this to be an omen of disaster to come.

It was impossible to continue the fight against the Cape Horn winds and seas, for, although conditions seemed favourable before the squall had hit the ship, she had only reached 70° west. Reluctantly they squared away and steered to the eastward. Because it would be necessary to get new topgallant and royal masts out from Britain it was decided to make for Montevideo in Uruguay. The winds would be in the ship's favour. The

Garthwray arrived there on the 9th December, 1922, after having been at sea for 140 days.

Repairs were carried out and then there was a wait for the masts to arrive. By the time they did the men in the fo'c'sle had deserted the ship and the nine apprentices had to carry out most of the work entailed in sending the old masts and yards down, sending the new ones up, and refitting the yards and gear to the new masts. It was a great experience for them, besides being invaluable when later they faced the seamanship examiner to obtain their second mate's certificate.

Captain John Henry, who was master of the *Garthforce* when she struck the iceberg was sent out by the owners to relieve Captain Mann. There seems to be some mystery about the second mate's movements, but he certainly left the ship in Montevideo on the 6th January, 1923, and, according to the Articles of Agreement, was not paid off. In his place Mr Siegfried Larsen, a Swede, aged 35, was signed on as second mate at £15 a month. The latter was hated. He was said to be a typical hard-case officer, who was particularly severe on the apprentices, usually finding them a 'work-up' job in the coffee watch, at half past five in the morning, when they should have been enjoying their coffee. His favourite stunt was pulling the buntlines on deck so breaking the twine buntline-stops underneath the blocks under the yards. The name given to the job thus made by the second mate was 'overhauling the buntlines' and it entailed going aloft and pulling up the buntlines (ropes) so that the rope on each side of the block through which they passed, could be tied together by twine. This held the weight and gave sufficient slack to the buntlines to prevent it lying tight against the sail, to which it was made fast, and so chafing it. When it became necessary to haul up the sail, by means of the buntlines, a sharp pull from the deck would break the twine holding the two parts under the block. This sharp pull was given uneccessarily by Mr Larsen before the apprentice was ordered to go aloft to do this 'worked-up' job.

His favourite punishment for apprentices who fell asleep while time-keeping on watch—ringing the poop bell a certain number of times at every half hour and hour—was to put a full bucket of water on one side of the poop and an empty one on the other. The water in one had to be transferred to the other with a teaspoon. This had to continue until the full bucket was emptied and invariably carried on well into the delinquent's watch below. But later when the kinder Mr Letts joined the ship as first mate he would release the apprentice long before the seemingly never-ending task was finished.

While in Montevideo the apprentices spent their spare time fishing, bathing and visiting British steamers in the port. Knowing how bad, and scarce, food was in the sailing ships, in which they had served their early years at sea, the steamship masters and officers never failed to invite the *Garthwray* lads on board to a meal or send food to them. No money was available for going on shore, but, at least, it was a respite from Cape Horn weather and all that it entailed in trying to make westing.

The ship was some four months in Montevideo and again sailed for Iquique on the 12th April, 1923. The ten new able seamen signed on proved good sailors, although they had been troublesome ashore in their drinking bouts. The Port and City Authorities were glad to get rid of them; the ship glad to get them.

The *Garthwray* once more attempted to round the 'Horn'. It seemed that there was still a hoodoo on the ship—perhaps a Jonah on board. If there was, then he must have been the first mate, one of the apprentices, or the carpenter, sailmaker or cook-steward. The rest of the crew and the master were new on board. It took 32 days to get down off the 'Horn' where the same weather was experienced, the same misery borne, and the same hopes unrealised. After the ship had battled against head gales and hurricane-force squalls she reached a position in latitude 58° 22′ south, longitude 70° west, on 22nd May—almost the same position where she had been damaged before—and in a squall of hurricane force accompanied by heavy hail and blinding snow, the main lower topsail yard truss, which connected the yard to the mast, carried away and left the yard hanging down over the lee side of the ship, in the sea, where, with the heavy rolling of the ship, the yard arm (the end of the yard) hammered dangerously against the hull.

The crew worked hard with knives and axes to clear it, doing their best to recover it and hoist it on board; and all the time mountainous seas crashed on board over the weather side, threatening to wash them all overboard. They were not successful and eventually had to let the yard sink into the sea. By then, everyone on board, from the first mate to the youngest apprentice, was exhausted. So a sea anchor was rigged with a storm mainsail and three spars lashed to its head and sides. Chain cables were made fast to each of the four corners of the sail and were shackled together in the centre in the form of a bridle to which a hawser was made fast for towing. It was put over the bow by means of a tackle rigged up on the fore yard arm. Then all sail was made fast and the ship lay comfortably, head-on to the seas, to the sea anchor, for two days. The author is of the opinion that a storm staysail would have been a better sail from which to make a sea anchor, but he was assured by one of the apprentices that it was made as he has described. It appears to have been thoroughly successful. Undoubtedly square-rigged sailing ships have used sea-anchors on similar occasions, but I have not heard or read of them.

When the weather improved it was found that in addition to the loss of the main lower topsail yard, the steel fore and main topmasts were fractured. Without the lower topsail yard the most vital sail in the ship in bad weather could not be set. Cape Horn had beaten the *Garthwray* once more. It was impossible to sail her into the Pacific, so the yards were squared and she sailed under reduced canvas before the wind to a port in distress.

The following lines were written by an old 'Cape Horner' who sailed round the dreaded 'Horn' eight times in British square-rigged sailing ships. It describes the passage round in the windjammers so well that I am impelled to include it in this 'Cape Horn' chapter.

We formed the crews who saw the last of sail,
The passing remnant of those better men
Who raced the clippers home, tea, passengers and mail,
That Golden Age now passed, and when
Their mantle fell on us, we did not fail.

Our ships were hard and heavy; in a trade
Those lovely wooden vessels never knew,
Close to Cape Horn the starboard tack was laid
Down to the ice. It blew! My God it blew!
But 'full and by' we to the westward made.

Came then the 'shift' to west-south-west; the breeze,
Eased up a little; oil bags put out
Giving the 'slick' which partly smoothed the seas
In which, as smartly as we could, we came about.
Hoping to clear the Diego Ramirez.

One, two, three weeks or four,
Sometimes when real unlucky even more;
Until we got the 'slant' and right away we bore
Up through the seas to Chile's western shore
Licking each and every Cape Horn sore.

These lines were written by Commander H W Green, who, on his first voyage as an apprentice in the barque *Powys Castle*, was wrecked on Staten Island, in January 1903, after the barque had rounded Cape Horn.

Captain Henry decided to make for Cape Town and after sailing across the South Atlantic, raised the light at Green Island on the 15th July, 1923. Then a head wind set the ship off shore and it was another five days before he contacted Signal Hill.

The Government tug *Ludwig Wiener* went out and towed the *Garthwray* into port on the 21st July, 1923, a year all but one day after leaving Grangemouth. She arrived with a list to port but fortunately had no sickness or accidents to the crew to report. The time taken from Montevideo to Cape Town was 100 days.

Repairs were carried out to the masts and a new main lower topsail yard was fitted in a week over two months. The apprentices would have liked a longer stay, for the people were so hospitable and kind to them. Cape Town was the home of Gray, one of the apprentices, so there were plenty of introductions, and as the ship was moored to a quay in the docks, shore-going was easy. They were invited out somewhere every evening and at the week-ends.

For me Cape Town has happy memories. I visited it when serving in the barque *Edinburgh*, owned by John Stewart & Co of London, many years before. The barque arrived there on Thursday and we were never given our weekly pocket money until Saturday. And that wasn't over much, even in those days; two shillings and sixpence for the first week and sixpence a week afterwards. So we made for the Missions to Seamen without a penny between us and were welcomed by the padre, the Rev G H E Collins. He greeted us with the fact that apart from the club facilities, always available, there was nothing special on that evening. He told our senior apprentice that there was an excellent concert at the Town Hall that night, and pressed the entrance money for us all into his hand. He knew the system of giving out pocket money by masters of sailing ships, and that we would certainly be broke that night. 'We'll have something here for you tomorrow night!' he added. He introduced us to many kind people in Cape Town who took us into their homes and on visits to the attractive scenic places outside Cape Town, including the top of Table Mountain. The Rev Collins was later a chaplain in the Royal Navy during the first world war, and later was the much-loved rector of the parish church at Rotherfield in Sussex. He was known as 'Cockatoo' Collins for he was often seen in the parish with his cockatoo perched on his shoulder. Great men, those Missions to Seamen padres! They did a wonderful job for the young apprentices, who were far from home, as well as for the seamen in the fo'c'sle. Nationality or religious denomination was no bar; everyone was welcome. And they visited our ships.

Captain Henry was afraid that the kindness of the good people ashore would prove too much for his seamen and apprentices, so, on the evening before the *Garthwray* was due to sail on one more attempt to get her cargo to Iquique, he stopped all shore leave in case they did not return to the ship. To make certain that no one left the ship he stationed a policeman on the gangway. This was a blow to the apprentices as they had been invited to a special farewell party. They worked out a plan.

The ship's raft was pulled under the jib boom at the bow of the ship, and, waiting until it was dark, they crept forward along the deck and, keeping out of sight of the policeman, went up on to the fo'c'sle head and out on the jib boom. Then they slid down a rope on to the raft and a couple of strokes with an oar brought them to the quay. They had a most enjoyable evening ashore and when they returned and walked boldly up the gangway, the policeman had the shock of his life.

Mr J M McLeod, the first mate, signed off the ship's articles at Cape Town on the 24th August, 1923 through illness. He was sent home and Mr E F Letts, who had been first mate of the *Garthsnaid* took his place, signing on the ship on the 17th August, 1923, at £17 a month. It will be noticed how the rate of pay was falling.

Captain Henry decided to have nothing more to do with Cape Horn on that passage, and, when the ship left on the 27th September, 1923, he sailed her down into the Roaring Forties and steered an easterly course round the world to the south of Tasmania and New Zealand with the fair westerly winds and gales. After crossing the South Pacific he set a course to the northward into the south-east trade winds and arrived at Iquique in 87 days, the best and fastest passage of all. Cape Horn had beaten the ship and her crew twice. She sailed into Iquique Bay on the 23rd December, 1923. The passage from Grangemouth had taken 519 days, the longest ever made by a windjammer, While in Iquique the indentures of some of the apprentices expired; they had completed their four years' apprenticeship. W R Hobden was promoted to third mate and Mr Dunn and others were signed on as sailors at £3.10s a month.

The cargo was discharged in good condition and ballast was taken on board. Orders were received for the ship to load a cargo of wheat at Talcahuano, South Chile, for Liverpool. The *Garthwray* left Iquique on the 15th March, 1924, and sailed to the westward, well out into the Pacific, to avoid the north-setting Humboldt Current. It was a fine weather passage and the crew took full advantage of the trade-wind weather. Iquique is not the best port in which to store a ship. Even so there were things in the store room aft that the apprentices would have dearly liked. Every Tuesday, when the ship was at sea, they took turns at scrubbing out the captain's rooms. On one occasion, during this passage, when it was Dunne's turn, the latter noticed that the store room door was open. So when he had finished the job, he slipped into the room, grabbed a tin of fruit, and dropped it into his bucket of dirty water. Unfortunately he didn't know that the captain was watching him through a mirror in the saloon. Young Dunne then went out on deck with his bucket; and the captain followed. As he started to go along the deck the captain asked him what he was going to do with the dirty water.

'Empty it in the scuppers for'ard, sir!' he said.

'Empty it in the scuppers, here!' ordered the captain.

There was no way of getting out of it so young Dunne tilted the bucket slightly so that the water ran out slowly. He hoped to be able to leave the tin in the bottom. But the captain was too wise for that, and he jogged Dunne's arm up and the tin fell out with a bang. He then picked it up and took it back to the saloon. Mr Dunne told me: 'Besides feeling so low at being caught that I could have walked under a snake with a top hat on, I had to spend the whole of my next watch below working on deck.' He never tried to 'win' a tin of fruit again.

Thirty-four days after leaving Iquique the ship was sailing in towards the coast to the south of Talcahuano. The weather had been misty and it had not been possible to get sextant sights to find the ship's position. Look-outs were stationed day and night.

It was at seven bells (11.20 am) on the morning of the 24th April, 1924, that young Dunne, having just been called for his dinner, was still in his bunk when he heard a German seaman, who was on the look-out, shouting from the bow of the ship. Captain Henry gave the order to square the cross-jack yard immediately, and all hands tumbled out on deck without waiting for the order.

The German had seen breakers ahead and within seconds the ship had driven on to the rocks. Cliffs could be discerned towering up through the heavy mist. The *Garthwray* was impaled on the rocks and it was soon seen that there was no possibility of getting her free. She was abandoned. The captain called to the apprentices to help him save the navigation instruments, log books and other ship's papers. One thing that was not saved—it found a watery grave—was the 'Slop Chest' Account Book. When it went over the side the record of all the parsimonious transactions of the voyage were lost. The 'slop chest' itself was popular enough but not the high prices charged.

The lifeboats were lowered and the crew rowed away well clear of the shore, for there was a heavy ground swell running which threatened to lift the boats on to the rocks and smash them to pieces. After rowing for five hours they came to a sandy beach where they landed and had a meal of corned beef and biscuits.

The *Garthwray* had stranded on the rocks off Santa Maria Island where she became a total loss. That evening a tug was sent over from Coronel to pick up the crew, but three of them, including Lionel Adams, were left on the island to see what could be salvaged from the ship. One thing they learnt while on the Island was to ride horses on wooden saddles. While there the *Garthwray* was broken up in a gale and there was nothing left to salvage. So the three joined the others at Coronel and they all went on to Valparaiso. Some were accommodated in a wing of the house of a millionaire and given the temporary use of a car with a chauffeur. But as they had no money the time spent there was described 'as a poverty-stricken week in luxury'. They joined the *Oropesa*, the Pacific Navigation Company's mail and passenger liner at Valparaiso and left there on the 24th May for home, arriving at Liverpool on the 13th June, 1924.

The *Invergarry* and *Garthgarry*

The *Invergarry* whose name was changed later to *Garthgarry* was a steel three-masted barque of 1,309 tons net. She was built by A McMillan & Son of Dumbarton in 1891 for George Milne & Company of Aberdeen. She was sold to William Brennand of Bank Chambers, Goole, Yorks, in 1917 for £16,000 and resold in 1918 to The Marine Navigation Company owned by William Garthwaite.

She had arrived at New York from Fremantle, Australia on the 21st May, 1918, but it was not until the 10th July that Mr Garthwaite's master, Captain J W Sharp, aged 65, from the Shetland Islands, signed on the ship's register as the *Invergarry*'s captain, having relieved Captain W M Macdonald, aged 28, of Auckland, New Zealand. Mr T Tennant of Dundee, who was then 66 years of age, carried on as first mate as did Mr R McIver, from Stornoway as second mate. He held a first mate's certificate and was 34.

When Captain Sharp arrived on board he found that Mr Tennant had nailed a writ to the door of the deck house—writs are usually fixed to the foremast—to prevent the ship from sailing until his wages were paid. This was most unusual; the author has never heard of another similar case.

Something else happened on board that is not easy to understand. It just seems as if someone was purposely being awkward. Tugs were ordered to shift the *Invergarry* from the pier and when they arrived it was found that neither the master nor the first mate was on board. It was not considered prudent to shift the ship and the tugs left without the job being carried out. The tug owners claimed a 'baulk' amounting to 90 dollars. This was compensation for the tugs because they were unable to carry out the job for which they were ordered. Either the owner or Captain Sharp, or perhaps both of them, considered Mr Tennant should have been on board to supervise the shifting of the *Invergarry*, and they sought to recover the 90 dollars by deducting it from Mr Tennant's wages. But it was not till the barque got to Melbourne months later, that it was entered into the Official Log Book and read over to Mr Tennant. He would not agree to the deduction and pointed out that Captain Sharp had no right to enter it into the Official Log Book as Captain Sharp's name was not on the ship's register as master when the incident happened, was not master of the ship then, and had no authority to act on behalf of the owners, or make the entry in the Official Log Book. As far as the author knows the 90 dollars was not deducted but it is sure that Mr Tennant was unpopular with his master and his owners.

The *Invergarry* had left New York, loaded, for Melbourne on the 20th July, 1918, and arrived on the 2nd December, 1918. There, Captain Francis Hodgens, aged 55, from Swansea, took over command from Captain Sharp. Grain was loaded for Callao, Peru, the barque leaving on the 31st January, 1919, and arriving on the 6th April. Another change was made in Callao. Mr Tennant was paid off and Mr Roderick MacIvor, having a first mate's certificate, was promoted to first mate and his wages increased to £20 a month. J Scully was signed on as second mate.

After the cargo had been discharged the *Invergarry* sailed in ballast for Mejillones to load nitrate for Durban. After she had left Mejillones, and was bound south to round Cape Horn, she met very bad weather in latitude 35° 10′ south, longitude 88° west, on the 14th July, 1919. The main deck was strained by heavy seas, the deck houses were damaged and leaked badly and the fresh water tanks were filled up with salt water owing to damage to the pipes. A number of sails were lost and several of the crew were laid up. Captain Hodgens decided to put into Talcahuano, Chile, in distress and the barque arrived there on the 22nd July, 1919. While there Alfred Ope succeeded J Scully as second mate. The *Invergarry* left Talcahuano on the 25th August, 1919, and arrived at Durban on the 17th October.

The next change of mates was when Mr McIver, first mate, left the barque in Durban, and Mr Stuart, aged 40, took his place. The *Invergarry* left Durban in ballast on the 4th November, 1919, for Newcastle, New South Wales, and there the voyage ended, the three years of their Agreement being finished, and all hands were paid off.

While the barque was in Newcastle her name was changed to *Garthgarry*. Her owners' address was given as The Marine Navigation Company of Canada Ltd, and her port of registry was changed to Montreal. The new crew signed on the barque on the 5th March, 1920, and she sailed for Iquique with a cargo of coals. After discharging her cargo she proceeded to Talcahuano in ballast to load for Durban where she arrived on the 10th February, 1921. She then sailed to Sydney in ballast. Here Captain H Aviss, aged 36, late master of the *Garthneill*, took over the command from Captain Hodgens. He had recently been in command of the yacht *Adventuress*, owned by Sir William Garthwaite as he was then. The first mate left here and was relieved by Mr C M Firth, aged 22, on the 13th July, 1921.

The *Garthgarry* loaded at Sydney for home and arrived at South Shields on the 28th December, 1921. The barque had been away for four years and ten and a half months, and during this time had four captains, four first mates, three second mates, and had changed her ownership and name: surely a record for any windjammer.

Captain Aviss was relieved by Captain David Roberts, a famous windjammer master who had come from the *Elginshire*. He was best known for the fast passages he made in the *Kirkcudbrightshire* of which he was master for twenty years. Although a strict disciplinarian he was a 'father' to his apprentices.

The *Garthgarry* loaded coal, briquettes and building bricks at North Shields and sailed for Port Louis, Mauritius on the 11th July, 1922. The name and address of her owners on the Crew Agreement was given as The Marine Navigation Company Limited, 5 Lloyds Avenue, London EC, and Messrs Everett & Company of the same address were her British agents. Her port of registry was recorded as Aberdeen. The author could never understand these changes. Mr William Wylie was her first mate. He had come from the *Garthpool* where he had been promoted to first mate on the death of Captain Atkinson when Mr Collins had taken over the command. Mr F W J Pearce was appointed second mate having come straight from the *Garthpool* with only three months to serve to complete his apprenticeship.

Mr Thomson came from the *Garthpool* to sail as third mate in the *Garthgarry*, and C E Carter and V Martin, who were apprentices in the *Garthforce* when she hit the iceberg, also joined her at North Shields. There were four other apprentices: Wise and Cole from Durban, H Watkins from Poole, Dorset, and one other, making six apprentices altogether.

The weather was reported as 'a moderate north-easterly wind with passing squalls and a nasty sea'. There was still wreckage pounding heavily against the hull of the barque and all hands worked at clearing it. At 2.30 next morning they were still working but had failed to save anything else, and, fearing that the spars which were pounding the sides of the barque might put a hole into her, Captain Roberts decided to let everything go overboard. Two hours later all the wreckage was clear of the barque.

The fore hatch had been stove in, the donkey engine was unseated and the spare fresh water tank damaged by 'flying' backstays. All the sails on the foremast, and the head sails and jibs, were gone. The fore lower cap was fractured and the crane of the lower topsail yard was bent. All the backstays and fore and aft stays on the foremast had gone overboard and the lower topsail yard was strained and bent. The foretop was completely destroyed and the bowsprit was fractured.

The fore upper topsail yard arm was lowered on to the fo'c'sle head and the yard was lashed outside the forward shrouds (the lower rigging). The yard was badly dented and bent and the parrel, which normally went round the mast and was attached to the yard, was lost. At 5 pm that day another foresail was bent on the fore yard and another fore lower topsail was also sent up. The water in the well had increased from four inches to ten inches in five hours so the pumps were rigged and worked all night, the crew gradually reducing the depth of water in the well.

On the next day, Monday the 24th March, 1924, the *Garthgarry* was in latitude 19° 22′ south, longitude 25° 23′ west at noon. The wind had dropped to a light east-north-east breeze but the sea was still rough and confused. An examination of the mainmast found that the main topmast head was strained and was working considerably. This had been caused by an excessive strain having been put on it by the fore and aft stays when the fore topmast came down. There was other damage of less importance. The broken bulwark stanchions could cause the loss of a section of the bulwarks and there were leaky rivets in the fore peak. These damages were repaired and the pumps were worked continuously with reliefs of four hands.

On the next night, Tuesday the 25th March, the crew were able to return to the ordinary sea watches after working continuously since the ship was dismasted. At noon that day the barque's position was latitude 17° 57′ south, longitude 26° 24′ west. The wind had settled to a moderate easterly breeze, the sea was moderate and the weather fine and cloudy. At six o'clock that morning a start had been made to send down the remaining portion of the fore topmast. Then the wooden mizzen topmast was sent down, ten feet cut off it, and it was hoisted up the foremast and secured to act as a jury fore topmast, and rigged with fore and aft stays and backstays. A three-inch steel wire was rigged from the mizzen lower mast head to the mainmast and an extra fore and aft sail was set on it. A double stay of this wire was also rigged from the fore lowermast head to the bowsprit and a fore staysail was set on that. At this time it was found that the well had been pumped dry, and, as no more water collected, pumping was stopped.

On the next day the fore topgallant yard was sent up and rigged on the jury fore topmast, lifts being fitted with 2½-inch wire from the mast above to the two ends of the yard. The sailmaker altered the upper topsail to fit the topgallant yard, and the sail was sheeted home on the lower topsail yard, there being no upper topsail yard there.

On Thursday the 27th March, the sail was sent up and all the gear was fitted to it ready for setting. On that day also the gear was rove on the lower topsail and foresail so that these sails could be set. On the next day, six days from the time of dismasting, strong lashings were put round the main topmast cap to the main topmast preventer backstays and frapping turns were taken and tightened up as much as possible. That was all that could be done at sea, and with that jury-rig, the barque sailed for Queenstown.

There is still something to say as to the cause of the disaster. Captain Roberts, it will be remembered, put it down to a squall. According to the information the author received from those serving on board at the time, including the second mate, whose watch it was when the accident occurred, there were two factors causing the dismasting.

The second mate took over the watch from the first mate at noon on the 22nd March when the barque was in the south-east trade winds. Going forward he saw that the new flying jib halliards were slack, as were the halliards of the other jibs, and the heads of the sails were also slack on the stays. So he ordered his watch to take a haul on the halliards to set the sails properly, which, of course, was his duty as the officer of the watch. After that he left Mr Benton, the third mate, to carry on with washing down the decks while he (the second mate) went aft to the saloon to dinner. He was about half way through the meal when he heard some rushing about on deck and went out immediately to see what it was all about. He saw 'the royal topgallant mast hanging upside down with the top of the royal mast touching the surface of the sea and the steel topmast jutting out forward from the lowermast at a forward angle'.

The second mate's opinion of the cause of the dismasting was that the steel topmast was rusted and that the weight on the masthead of that extra flying jib set on the royal stay was too much for it. Although the second mate insisted on Captain Roberts being a good seaman it was his opinion that it was asking a lot of the foremast of an old barque to carry an extra 'top'—flying jib—in a stiff breeze.

The apprentices were certain that the cause of the dismasting was firstly that the mast was rusted through, and secondly that hauling on the flying jib halliards put additional strain on it.

The *Garthgarry* arrived at Queenstown on the 6th June, 1924, after a long passage of 149 days. She stayed there at anchor for a week and then was towed to Barrow-in-Furness to discharge her cargo, arriving on the 15th June. Here she was sold to shipbreakers for £2,000 and was broken up.

The *Inverneill* and *Garthneill*

The *Inverneill* was another of George Milne's handy and pretty steel, three-masted barques. Built by Russell & Company of Port Glasgow in 1895 her net tonnage was 1,340. Mr William Garthwaite bought her when she was in Bilbao, Spain, in July 1916, for £13,000, her new ownership being registered as The Marine Navigation Company Limited, 92/94 Gracechurch Street, London EC. She sailed for New York in ballast on the 3rd August, 1916, arriving on the 12th September. Captain Herbert Aviss, of Coventry, 32 years of age, who held an extra master's certificate was her master and his wife, who was then 26, sailed with him. She was the elder daughter of Captain Frampton of the *Wray Castle* and *Garthwray*. Mr J H Shippen, aged 34, of Maryport, Cumberland, was the first mate and Mr L Pigott, aged 22, of Prince Edward Island, Canada, was signed on as bosun and acted as second mate.

In New York Mr Shippen signed off the *Inverneill* and was appointed master of Mr Garthwaite's barque *Carnmoney* on the 28th September. His wife joined him at Norfolk, Virginia, and signed on the *Carnmoney* as stewardess. As has been related the *Carnmoney* was later sunk by a German submarine. Mr G A Smith signed on the *Inverneill* at New York as first mate on the 22nd October, 1916. He was a Londoner, aged 25, and held a first mate's certificate. Two days later the barque left with a full cargo for Melbourne, arriving on the 31st January, 1917. Mr Smith paid off there on the 8th February and Mr T J Harris, aged 44, of Nelson, New Zealand, signed on as first mate at £18 a month.

The *Inverneill* left Melbourne on the 21st March, 1917 with a cargo of wheat for Bordeaux where she arrived safely on the 17th July. Here Mr Harris left and Captain Shippen of the *Carnmoney*, which had been sunk by submarine on the 14th May, took his place as first mate at £20 a month. At this time the *Inverneill* was recorded in Lloyd's Register of Shipping as being owned by The Marine Navigation Company of Canada Limited, registered at Montreal. No doubt she wore the Canadian Merchant Navy flag. Her name still remained *Inverneill*.

She sailed from Bordeaux on the 30th September for Port Arthur in Texas and arrived there on the 19th November, 1917. Here she loaded for Sydney, Australia, leaving the Sabine Pass Roads on the 26th December, 1917 and arriving on the 19th April, 1918. Mr Pigott, the second mate, left the ship at Port Arthur.

Wheat was loaded at Sydney for St John, New Brunswick, Canada, the barque leaving on the 23rd May, 1918 and arriving on the 7th October. On this passage Captain and Mrs Aviss's second child was born at sea on the 27th August at 3.15 pm in latitude 3° 30′ south, longitude 32° 15′ west. It was a daughter whom they named Ruth Neill. The entry in the Official Log stated: 'Both mother and daughter doing well' signed by Herbert Aviss, master and J H Shippen, mate. Mrs Aviss also had a son named Ronald who had been born at sea in the *Inverneill* on the 26th April, 1915. She herself had been born at sea in a windjammer of which her father, Captain Frampton, was master.

What plucky women those windjammer captain's wives were. It was impossible to know what weather their ships would be experiencing when the time came for their confinements. And what anxiety for their husbands, who had to be midwife and doctor. They would have what assistance could be given by the first mate and steward; but there was rarely another woman on board. In the case of Mrs Aviss the weather was fine in the tropics; but it was probably unbearably hot.

When the *Inverneill* arrived at St John it was learned by her master and crew that the world-wide epidemic of Spanish Influenza had reached the port. Fourteen seamen and Mrs Aviss fell victims to it and were taken to hospital. One seaman and Mrs Aviss died. Her death, reported to be from pneumonia, took place on the 3rd November, 1918. What a tragedy! Captain Aviss was left with the young baby, not three months old, and his little son aged three. He went home with both the children and the first mate, Mr Shippen, took over the command of the *Inverneill* on the 23rd November, 1918. Mr F L Coe, aged 32, of Liverpool, signed on as first mate on the same day.

A full cargo was loaded for Melbourne and the barque sailed on the 6th December arriving on the 26th April, 1919. Here Mr Coe left the barque on the 6th June and Mr R W Ronald, aged 50, joined as first mate at £26 a month. He came from Greenwich, London. At Melbourne Captain Shippen received orders to sail in ballast to Bunbury, Western

Australia, to load jarrah wood sleepers for Cape Town. While in Melbourne it was reported that the prefix *Inver* had been replaced by *Garth* in her name painted on each bow and on the counter. This is the only mention, so far, of the barque's change of name to *Garthneill*. In fact she does not appear in her official papers as *Garthneill* until 1921. If this painting of the new name was indeed carried out, it was altered back to *Inverneill*.

Bunbury is less than 2,000 miles from Melbourne by sea, but the barque, being in ballast and meeting strong westerly gales and heavy head seas, could not beat across the Great Australian Bight. The *Inverneill* left Melbourne on Sunday the 6th July, 1919, and that night off Cape Otway the wind, which had been blowing from the north-west during the day, went round to the south-west and increased to gale force. The barque sailed through the Bass Strait, but, ten days later she was off the southern end of Tasmania facing gales blowing from north-west to west with no possibility of making westing. Captain Shippen decided to run for Sydney where he arrived on the 29th July. He anchored in Double Bay.

The barque sailed again on the morning of the 14th August when a moderate westerly wind was blowing. Before the evening the wind freshened to a south-south-westerly gale and, after consulting Mr R W Ronald, his first mate, Captain Shippen decided to make the passage to the eastward, right round the world, with the fair westerly winds of the Roaring Forties and Howling Fifties (40° and 50° south latitude). He sailed the barque to the southward of Cape Horn and the Cape of Good Hope.

The *Inverneill* passed the northernmost tip of New Zealand when five days out from Sydney; Cape Horn when thirty-three days out and St Paul's Island in the South Indian Ocean when sixty-six days out. In another ten days the barque had arrived in Bunbury, the passage having taken seventy-six days from Sydney. The distance recorded by the ship's patent log was 14,563 miles, an average of 191.6 miles a day. Her best day's run was 300 miles. In the barque's favour was the fact that she was sailing in ballast and had recently come out of dry dock.

The weather was very bad during most of the passage. At times the gales were so heavy that the *Inverneill* had to be hove-to and lie head to wind without making any progress. Snow squalls were experienced and, at times, ice formed on the rigging. It was continuous bad weather for two and a half months with no let-up; or even a chance to dry out wet clothes and limp oilskins. It is easy to understand the anxiety of Captain Shippen to make as fast a passage as possible after deciding that sailing fourteen and a half thousand miles with a fair wind was a better proposition than attempting two thousand miles with a probable head wind all the way. Of course he might have had a let-up and been able to break through; but who could tell! He probably would have chosen to do this if the *Inverneill* had been loaded. But Captain Shippen never had any doubt that he had made the right decision. When he arrived at Bunbury he learnt that the winds had been blowing strong from the westward for three months. He remembered the case of a loaded barque, a few years before, that took seventy-five days from Melbourne to Albany, Western Australia, in the winter months. And the author must stress how the loaded barque, deeper in the water, has a better grip than the barque flying light; and how the latter will be beaten back by the wind blowing on her more exposed hull much higher out of the water.

The *Inverneill* arrived at Bunbury on the 29th October, 1919 and loaded jarrah wood sleepers for Cape Town. She left on the 26th November and arrived on the 17th January, 1920. Here Mrs Shippen joined her husband. The barque left Cape Town in ballast to return to Bunbury on the 12th February. She arrived on the 26th March, loaded another cargo of jarrah wood sleepers, and left again on the 24th April, this time for Durban where she arrived on the 9th June. These passages are probably the easiest of any for a windjammer. Sailing across the South Indian Ocean from Australia to South Africa she would sail before the wind in the south-east trades and in tropical weather. Returning she would sail down to the south and get the benefit of the strong westerly winds and gales in the Roaring Forties.

This time the *Inverneill*, after discharging her sleepers, loaded coal for Port Louis, Mauritius, leaving Durban on the 15th July and arriving at Mauritius on the 14th August. When her coals had been unloaded, she took in ballast and sailed on the 28th September, back once again to

Bunbury where she arrived on the 23rd October, 1920. Here Mr Ronald, the first mate, left her and Mr Harold E Mackenzie took his place. He was 43 years of age and came from Warminster in Wiltshire. His pay was £28 a month, but he only made one short passage in her, across to Cape Town where he paid off on the 7th February, 1921. The next first mate was Mr S H Warriner, aged 30, from Loughton, Essex.

Captain and Mrs Shippen also left the barque in Cape Town at this time and went home. Captain David Thomson came out from home and relieved Captain Shippen, on the 7th March, 1921.

Captain David Thomson was one of the most famous and successful of all the windjammer captains. He spent the whole of his sea service in square-rigged sailing ships following his father who was also a capable sailing ship master. This was his first command in the ships and barques of Sir William Garthwaite. He was then 55 years of age. Captain J W Broadhouse, a New Zealander, who joined the barque later in Dunedin, described his Captain as: 'A Scot as broad in speech as he was in stature; a splendid seaman and as fine a sailmaker as there was to be found outside a sailmaker's loft. He came from Anstruther in Fifeshire and was born in 1866. He went to sea when sixteen years of age. His father, Captain James Thomson from St Andrews, went to sea in 1845 and served fifty years in sailing ships.

Captain David Thomson served as third, second and first mate of the *Euphrosyne* when his father commanded her, and, when the latter retired, he took over the command in 1895 when 29 years of age. He was also master of the windjammers *Lauriston*, *Vimiera*, *Hinemoa* and *Milverton* before being appointed to the command of the *Inverneill*. He was to be the last captain of a British windjammer.

The *Inverneill* sailed from Cape Town to Bunbury in ballast and here the voyage, which started on the 23rd May, 1918 in Sydney, finished and the crew were paid off on the 7th May, 1921, when the three-year period of the barque's Articles of Agreement for the officers and crew terminated. The new Articles were opened on the 9th May, 1921. Mr Warriner remained as first mate at £26 a month and Mr J de Vos, aged 26, a Dutch seaman, signed on as bosun and second mate at £18 a month.

He was known on board as 'Dutchy' Voss, was an excellent officer and seaman and popular with everyone on board.

The new Articles of Agreement still gave the barque the name of *Inverneill* which was changed, soon after they were opened, to *Garthneill.* This latter name was then painted on the bow and the stern of the ship, and her new port of registry, Montreal, was painted under her name on the stern. What is not easy to understand is why *Inverneill* remained painted on the lifeboats, lifebuoys and fire buckets.

She loaded a full cargo of jarrah wood sleepers for Dunedin, New Zealand, where they were discharged at the old Birch Street Wharf. Here young Broadhouse, now Captain J V Broadhouse of Auckland, New Zealand, joined her as an ordinary seaman one blustery August morning in 1921. Like the other barques and ships in the Company her hull was painted a French grey colour with white deck work and teak-coloured masts and yards. She had a full fo'c'sle head and poop and two houses on the main deck. Captain Broadhouse described her as a happy and lucky ship, which is about as favourable a description of his ship as a seaman could give.

There was a very mixed crowd of sailors in the fo'c'sle, including the son of a British Consul in the United States, Canadians, Americans, Scandinavians and a native from Mauritius, but they were all good shipmates and a friendly atmosphere pervaded the fo'c'sle.

After the sleepers had been discharged, about 600 tons of clay was taken on board. To prevent it shifting from side to side shifting boards were lashed longitudinally to the stanchions amidships in the holds where the ballast was stowed. In the event they were unnecessary because the clay set solidly and pickaxes had to be used when it was discharged at Geelong, near Melbourne.

It was about the 28th August, 1921, when the *Garthneill* was towed to sea by the tug *Dunedin.* Sail was set and the barque made to the northward to a fresh, south-easterly wind. Captain Thomson intended to sail round the North Island, but, on reaching Cook Strait, between the South and North Island, the wind shifted and blew a moderate gale from the north-west. A week was spent wearing ship from tack to tack every four hours and the barque was set to the eastward. When the fair wind came a course was set through Cook Strait into the Tasman Sea. Bad weather and head winds were met there and it was not till about the 17th September that the *Garthneill* was towed into Geelong to load a cargo of bagged wheat for Durban. Young Broadhouse's job was in the lower holds where he bled the tops of the bags with his sheath knife to fill the gaps in the stowage with loose grain to make a solid stowage and increase the weight in the lower holds for stability purposes. At Geelong Mr Edward Harrison, aged 52, who came from Hull, was signed on as first mate in the place of Mr Warriner on the 3rd October, 1921, at £27 a month. At the end of October the barque was towed out over the rip at the entrance to Port Phillip Bay and started her beat against a head wind across the Great Australian Bight. She was lucky with winds later and rounded Cape Leuwin to make her northing into the fine weather of the south-east trade winds. Here, on the dry decks, Captain Thomson was able to carry on with his skilful and useful hobby of sailmaking. He had the hands, most useful with a sail needle and palm, aft with him on the poop and after main deck which was arrayed with bolts of canvas, skeins of twine, palms and needles, sailmakers' benches and all the paraphernalia associated with the making and repairing of sails. The whole set up was known as the 'Old Man's sewing-bee'. He sat in the middle of the five or six seamen and with the sailmaker set the pace of stitching. He was 55 years of age then, but made every sail in the ship from the huge, heavy courses (main and fore sails) to the lighter canvassed royals as well as the storm staysails, jibs and smaller flying kites at the top of the masts. And he would go aloft in fine weather some 150 feet up the mast to repair a royal to save unbending it and sending it down on to the deck.

The barque arrived at Durban early in January, 1922 and, a month later, the cargo had been discharged, ballast had been taken in, and she was down in the 'Roaring Forties' on her way to Semaphore, Port Adelaide. But the westerly gales did not live up to their reputation. It was summertime down there and it was not until early in April that the *Garthneill* arrived at the Wonga Shoal anchorage in St Vincent's Gulf. Three weeks were spent at anchor off Semaphore and the orders came through for the barque to proceed to Newcastle, New South Wales. While at Semaphore Mr Harrison, first mate, signed off and Mr Macdonald, aged 48, of Glasgow joined in his place at £25 a month on the 6th April, 1922.

It was on a clear moonlight Sunday evening that the barque got under way. The flood tide was turning to the ebb, and a north-westerly wind was blowing when the crew hove-up the anchor, trudging round the capstan on the fo'c'sle head to the tune and time of several capstan shanties. Then they hoisted the upper topsail yards with the help of halliard shanties, and the barque headed down the Gulf to Kangaroo Island. Later they heard that they had provided an evening's entertainment to the people on the Semaphore sea front as they watched the barque sail past the Wonga Shoal Light and heard the singing across the water. Young Broadhouse was now an able seaman, having been promoted the previous day.

The *Garthneill* arrived at Newcastle at the beginning of May and berthed at the jetties at Upper Stockton where she lay for over a month waiting her turn to load. It was well into the middle of June before she was towed to sea from the Farewell Buoy, deeply loaded with coals for Callao, Peru. Since the wind was coming from the south-east, Captain Thomson decided to sail to the north of New Zealand. The barque started from the Nobby's (entrance to Hunter River, Newcastle) at ten knots, and, two days later, as the approach was made to Cape Marda van Diemen (north-west point of New Zealand), the wind fell light and the 'Old Man' started his 'sewing bee'. About ten o'clock in the morning that day, what appeared to be an open boat was sighted about two points (22½ degrees) on the starboard bow, about three miles distant. Course was altered to pass close and it was found to be the derelict after-part of the American schooner, *Helen B Sterling*, which had been dismasted the previous week. A New Zealand naval ship had taken the crew off, and, weather conditions preventing the schooner being towed, bombs had been placed in her holds to sink her. As she was loaded with timber the attempt at sinking her had not been altogether successful and about half of her was still afloat. The *Garthneill* had no wireless, and, not meeting a steamer, could not report the derelict until she arrived at Callao.

It was no record passage that the barque was making across the South Pacific for it was not until the second week in August that the island of San Lorenzo was sighted and the barque was towed to an anchorage in Callao by the small tug, *El Paso*.

The day the *Garthneill* arrived a holiday fiesta was being held ashore, and the populace, seeing the barque approaching from the sea, concluded it was the one they were waiting for to save them from starvation. They prepared a red-carpet, brass-band reception for the crew; but when the cargo carried was found to be coals the whole reception was abandoned. A week later the barque *Birkdale* arrived from Melbourne with the cargo of wheat and the senoritas turned on the grand reception for the crew who had broken their famine—much to the disgust of the coal carriers.

By the end of the month the cargo of coals had been discharged at a berth in the dock and 200 tons of ballast taken in the main lower hold. In the event this was not enough to put the barque down sufficiently in the water for the purpose of handling her in a breeze of wind. The tug *El Paso* was sent to tow her to Mazorca Island, 80 miles from Callao, where she was to load 2,000 tons of guano for a British or European port. It appears that the small tug was towing alongside amidships and acting as main engines for the *Garthneill*, for, when the barque was rounding the breakwater, a gust of wind caught her hull and top-hamper (masts, yards, rigging etc) and blew her down on to the mole. Unfortunately the *El Paso* was between the barque and the mole and she was crushed, dented and holed, and her decks were buckled. She had to return for repairs and the *Garthneill* anchored in the Bay.

Two high-powered launches were sent out to the *Garthneill* to resume the towage. Assisted by an off-shore wind, the barque started her eighty miles passage with the two launches towing ahead and her topsails set. At midnight the launch towing on the port bow stopped, drifted astern, and then brought up suddenly on her tow rope. Her lights vanished and she rolled over and sank. The other launch slipped her tow-rope and went back to pick up survivors, but all they found was a couple of empty oil drums. Three men had lost their lives because they had not slipped the tow-rope of their launch when the engines broke down. The tow-rope had tightened up as the barque went ahead and rolled the launch over.

The other launch, with the help of the barque's sails, towed the ship to Mazurka Island which is in latitude 11° 24′ south, longitude 77° 44′ west. It is the largest of the Huaura Group of islets and is 272 feet high with a conical summit yellow with guano. Captain Broadhouse described it as a 'God-forsaken hole; a tall rocky outcrop in the middle of the ocean, smothered with birds, birds and more birds, a type of shag which the natives called "guanai".' There was no vegetation there. The *Garthneill* lay at anchor in an open roadstead. Six lighters brought the guano from the island out to the ship and the crew hove it on board and stowed it in the holds. This took a month to complete; some 2,000 tons of it. It is, of course, bird droppings accumulated over many years; an acrid, evil-smelling cargo. Working down in the close atmosphere and heat of the holds—it was only 11½ degrees from the equator—the guano brought on nose bleeding which could, it was claimed, be stopped by drinking a local white wine called vino-piser. Captain Broadhouse said that judging from the smell, taste and kick it was probably methylated spirits.

It was a happy day when the crew put on the hatches and tarpaulins, and hove-up the anchors short, so that they could get the remaining anchor cable and the anchor right up early on the next morning. They were bound for Hull and as they sailed south to Cape Horn the backstays and shrouds slackened and had to be set up. I have not carried guano so have not experienced this. The explanation given by Captain Broadhouse is that the tops of the barque's side plating were bending inboard due to the cargo of guano being wet when loaded, and, drying out at sea, settled down so increasing the weight at the bottom of the hold. This also set up excessive and lively rolling which lasted for the whole passage.

Bad luck was met off Cape Horn where they encountered head winds for a week in the form of south-easterly gales. During this time kalashi watches were kept, which meant that both watches were standing by for the whole twenty-four hours of the day. When they had a chance to try and snatch a little sleep they had to lie down in their oilskins and seaboots. Both half deck and fo'c'sle were washed out by heavy seas, and the only dry place was the sail locker which all the deck hands and apprentices occupied.

While sailing north to the fine weather of the tropics a serious leak was found in the main fresh water tank. It was plugged but it meant that the fresh water ration was cut to a quart of rusty sludge per man per day. Slow progress was made to the northward, partly caused by lack of wind and partly to the foul bottom of the barque.

The approach to the English Channel was made by dead reckoning for no sights had been possible for four days. Luckily, about eight o'clock in the morning, a trawler, the *Roche Castle*, steamed out of the fog and gave the 'Old Man' the bearing and distance off the Lizard. But it took another week to sail up the Channel and the North Sea to Spurn Head where a tug was taken and the pilot boarded.

At 6 pm on the 12th February, 1923, the *Garthneill* berthed in the Tidal Basin, Hull, and the voyage finished. The port anchor had been dropped to prevent her falling heavily on her berth, and, when the tide fell, the fluke of the anchor went through her plating into the fore peak which was flooded. On the next morning the crew were paid off at the Shipping Office.

The next voyage started at Hull on the 15th March, 1923, the *Garthneill* then being towed to Middlesborough to load coals for Port Louis, Mauritius. When loaded she sailed on the 10th April, her owners being given as The Marine Navigation Company of Canada, Limited, the barque being registered at Montreal. Captain Thomson remained in her as master and Mr W Loades, aged 60, who came from Salcombe in Devon, was her new first mate. His wages were £15 a month, considerably less than the wages paid out in Australia. He had come from the *Garthforce* where he had been serving as second mate. He had a master's square-rigged certificate and, it was said, had been in command of a big four-masted barque.

Although J Duly signed on as bosun at £11.10s a month, as far as the author can find out, J de Vos (Dutchy) sailed as second mate. The able seamen were paid £10 a month and the ordinary seamen £3.10s a month. Besides the apprentices, a cadet signed on at 6s 8d a month.

On the passage out to Mauritius the *Garthneill* met with the most terrific gales that Captain Thomson had ever met in his long experience in windjammers, which goes to prove that the worst weather is not always to be found off Cape Horn. The *Garthneill* was down to the southward of the Cape of Good Hope. The two lifeboats were completely smashed and deck fittings were washed overboard by mountainous seas. The doors of the fo'c'sle and the deck houses were smashed in. The sea-water even got down into the lazarette under the after saloon and ruined the store of flour.

The *Garthneill* arrived at Port Louis on the 26th June, 1923 and sailed in ballast for Cape Borda at the western end of Kangaroo Island on the 7th September. But bad weather made it impossible to signal the lighthouse keeper at Cape Borda and Captain Thomson had to carry on with his barque under two lower topsails. He reported to an Adelaide newspaper:

> We sailed through the passage between the Scraper and Cape St Albans without a particle of danger. My ship *Garthneill* drawing only 11 feet 6 inches and there was 30 feet of water under her. The channel was about a quarter of a mile wide and we were running before the wind with topsails and topgallant sails set. It was necessary to approach close to Cape Willougby (at eastern end of Kangaroo Island) so that our signal could be read by the lighthouse keeper.

Orders were received to proceed to Newcastle, New South Wales, and the *Garthneill* arrived there on the 30th October, 1923. Incidentally this wonderful navigation through a passage only a quarter of a mile wide was a great achievement for any sailing ship master and I doubt if it was done very often. The barque loaded coals in Newcastle for Tocopilla, Chile, and she left on the 2nd December, 1923, arriving on the 4th February, 1924. There were no nitrate cargoes available for the *Garthneill* in the Chilian ports and she sailed back to Sydney in ballast arriving there on the 21st June. Contrary to expectation there were no wheat cargoes for windjammers there, and the barque sailed to Newcastle once again for another cargo of coals which she loaded for Taltal. Even so she had to wait nearly a month for it and did not leave until the 1st August.

She arrived there on the 14th September, and received orders to sail for Iquique on the 20th September to discharge her coal and load nitrate. She arrived on the 27th September and left, loaded for London, on the 22nd November, 1924.

It was a slow passage down the Pacific to Cape Horn and it took 75 days to reach a position off the Falkland Islands in the South Atlantic. The barque passed so close to them that they could be seen through the mist and driving spray. Captain Thomson seemed to prefer to pass close to land. It may have been an urge to verify his position, or it may be that his ship was always set in towards land. He was certainly a good navigator.

After this the *Garthneill*'s progress improved for she arrived at Gravesend, London River, on the 28th March and entered Millwall Dock on the 1st April, 1925. There she discharged her cargo, the crew being paid off on her arrival. On the 14th May, she was towed down river to anchor in Gravesend Reach, and on the 2nd June went alongside the Thurrock Chalk Pier to take in 75 tons of cast iron scrap as ballast.

The new crew signed on at Tilbury on the 25th May, Captain Thomson remaining as master and Mr Loades as first mate at £15.10s a month. 'Dutchy' Vos signed on as second mate at £11.10s a month. The able seaman's wage stood at £10 a month.

At this time there were only four British windjammers trading. They were John Stewart's *Monkbarns* and *William Mitchell* and the Marine Navigation Company of Canada's *Garthneill* and *Garthpool*. Besides apprentices there were five cadets signed on the *Garthneill* for the voyage at £2 a month. They included three Australians and one from Great Britain from the four-masted barque *Bellpool* which had been sold. The *Garthneill* lay at anchor in the Gravesend Reach, London River, until the 9th June, 1925.

Captain Frank Walker joined the *Garthneill* for this voyage as an Ordinary Seaman on the 22nd May, 1925. He was a Gravesend, Kent, boy who now lives in Waveland, Mississippi, in the United States of America. At the time of writing he is serving as master in the Delta Steamship Lines Inc, of New Orleans. After leaving the *Garthneill* he joined the *Garthpool* and in December 1934 obtained his British master's certificate, with square-rigged endorsement, and joined the Cunard Line.

He also holds a licence as Master Unlimited, in the United States of America. During the Second World War he served in the Royal Naval Reserve and rose to the rank of Commander.

The *Garthneill* left Gravesend Reach for Grangemouth on the 10th June and arrived on the 25th June. The barque was becalmed in the North Sea for three days surrounded by fishing trawlers. Bumboats, once known as copers, were supplying cheap liquor to the fishing boats during the dark hours, and, unknown to Captain Thomson, the bumboat men boarded the barque and made sales to the men in the fo'c'sle. Two vessels from the Fishermen's Mission, the Royal National Mission to Deep Sea Fishermen, were also boarding the trawlers, holding services and bringing comforts and medical aid to the fishermen. The missioners also boarded the *Garthneill* and held a service on the main deck which was attended by all hands. They had their own musical instruments and a portable organ for accompanying the hymns. Some members of the crew had accordions and they joined in with the accompaniments. After the service Captain Thomson entertained the missioners in the saloon aft. When they left they gave the Captain a considerable quantity of woollen goods, scarves, mittens, gloves, seaboot hose, jerseys and leather gloves for distribution to the crew. This is the only occasion on which I have heard of a service held in a windjammer at sea by a Mission.

The *Garthneill* loaded coke at Grangemouth for Melbourne leaving on the 7th July 1925. On the 19th September the barque had arrived in latitude 41° 23′ south, longitude 4° 53′ east and was encountering fresh winds and squalls of hail and sleet. One of the royals had split badly, and had been replaced, when some seams of the fore upper topsail blew adrift. To save sending that sail down it was hauled up and Captain Thomson, assisted by young Walker, went aloft to repair it. No easy job with a sea running and the barque rolling and pitching; and Captain Thomson was 59 years of age.

The *Garthneill* arrived at Melbourne on the 5th November after a passage of 121 days. She was chartered to carry the coke by Messrs Agad, Forster and Parker of London and it was said that the owners lost money on the passage.

When the cargo had been discharged no other cargoes were on offer so she sailed to Adelaide on the 25th July where she was sold to become a wheat storage hulk on the 10th August, 1926. Captain Thomson and her first and second mates stayed with her until she was handed over to the new owners on the 10th August. 'Dutchy' de Vos stayed on board as ship-keeper and Captain Walker went on board in 1927 to see him in his neat little nautical home in the captain's and officers' quarters. He was then married and had a very young baby.

Commander Alan Villiers, DSC, the well-known nautical author, visited the *Garthneill* later. He saw 'houses strewn about her decks and bits of elevators poking out of her holds, and her stumps of masts being used to swing derricks. And her figure head, a pretty Scots lass, still there but rusty and mournful.'

When Captain Broadhouse, who it will be remembered sailed in her from August 1921 to February 1923, visited Adelaide later, before the Second World War, he found that her figure head had gone and her stem had been cut away. She had lost her bowsprit, her masts had been cut down to her lowermasts and a corrugated iron construction had been built up on the forward deck house to shelter the donkey engine.

Captain Broadhouse walked forward to what had been her fo'c'sle, a house between the fore and main masts, where he had lived as an ordinary and able seaman for eighteen months. In this time on board there had been seven individual compartments in the fo'c'sle house; two fo'c'sles, two mess rooms, the galley and two double berth cabins for the cook and the ordinary seamen. Now it was one compartment littered with coal, ashes, old rope, empty cases and sawn-off derricks. With two exceptions all the doorways had been boarded up, most of the glass ports were broken, and the deckhead (roof) had been removed and replaced by a corrugated iron canopy.

He went straight to a corner where the shelf which had held his books used for studying for his second mate's examination was still there. The half deck, where the apprentices had lived, was in no better condition. It was knee-deep in rubbish although some of the bunk fittings were still there. But the captain's and officers' cabins and the saloon had not altered from their seafaring days. In the second mate's cabin the wooden bunk had been taken away and a brass bedstead had been installed in its place. Curtains were up at the ports, there were flowers on the saloon table and pictures on the bulkheads (walls). It was still the home of the ship-keeper, his wife, and at least one in the family.

There was one thing remaining on board from the *Garthneill*'s sailing days—the hard, leather-topped settee in the chart room on the poop deck which the captain used in bad weather. Something new were flower pots containing flowering plants on the seats on either side of the saloon skylight on the poop. Captain Broadhouse walked right aft to the wheel and looked at its midship spoke. His initials, deeply carved into the wood, were still there. This, he remembered, he had done one fine afternoon in the trade winds when the first mate had gone forward to see how his watch were getting on with the job he had set them.

The *Garthneill* was by no means finished as an ocean sailing vessel when she was hulked. She was in a wonderful condition for her thirty-one years. It was just that there were no longer cargoes that would pay British wind-jammers to carry. Now the *Garthpool* alone remained in the fleet and the only cargo available for her was wheat which Sir William Garthwaite bought in Australia and carried home in her.

The *Juteopolis*

The *Juteopolis*, a four-masted, stump topgallant barque of 2,652 tons net, carried a deadweight cargo of 4,450 tons. She was the last British windjammer, her name being changed to *Garthpool* some time after she was bought by William Garthwaite in 1917. The name *Juteopolis* was taken from her home port, Dundee, the jute city. She was first engaged in the jute trade between Calcutta and Dundee and was built in 1891 at Dundee by Messrs Thompson and Company for Charles Barrie of Dundee who owned the Dundee-Calcutta Line. At the time of her building, windjammers were having difficulty in competing with steamers and were designed for the utmost economy in maintenance, manning and operation. Compared with the fine-lined tea and wool clippers they were long steel boxes designed to carry as much cargo as possible on as light a draft as convenient.

The *Juteopolis* did not altogether comply with this box-like structure principle. She was certainly full amidships but she was fine in the entrance and had a clean run aft. Her holds were available entirely for cargo except for the space taken up by the fresh water tanks. She had, like other windjammers, only one watertight bulkhead, which was at the fore end of No 1 hold on the after side of the fore peak.

She had a raised fo'c'sle right forward, a raised poop right aft and a raised superstructure amidship, usually known as a Liverpool House, but on board the *Juteopolis* was called the Midship Section. This contained quarters for the seamen, the petty officers and apprentices and also contained the sail locker, galley and donkey house. This latter housed the donkey boiler which supplied steam for raising the anchor and hoisting the heavier sails. It was rarely used at sea.

The half deck, or the apprentices' quarters, in the midship house measured twenty-four feet by nine feet and contained ten bunks, a table, two benches and a paraffin lamp. Clothes were kept in sea chests in front of the bunks. Bedding, enamel plates, mugs and cutlery were provided by the apprentices. There were two fo'c'sles for the seamen, having twelve bunks in each. Access for apprentices and seamen was by scuttles and ladders leading down from the top deck as well as by passages leading in from main deck doors. This was a great help in keeping this accommodation dry and avoiding seas flooding it in bad weather, as was the case of deck houses with doors opening on to the main deck.

Under the fo'c'sle head, in the bows of the barque, were the lamp room, paint locker, bosun's store and lavatories. There were no wash houses; buckets were used for baths in what shelter could be obtained when necessary. There was no seclusion.

The captain and mates were accommodated right aft under the poop. Each mate had his own room and they had their own mess room apart from the saloon where the captain had his meals. There was a fine large teak deckhouse on the poop which housed the chart room and led down to the saloon and the captain's and mates' rooms. Her double wheel was right aft on the poop in an open-fronted wheel house. The stores, including the food for all hands, were kept in the lazarette under these quarters.

The rig of the *Juteopolis* was designed for easy handling and for driving her in strong winds. She had the handy jubilee-rig more commonly known as stump topgallant or bald-headed. With this rig the lower and upper topgallant sails were larger than were usually set at the top of the topgallant mast. The height of her masts from main deck to truck (the top) was 156 feet. The fore, main and mizzen masts, carried the square sails on their yards and each similar yard was interchangeable on each mast. Her topgallant masts and yards were of wood; all other masts and yards were of steel. Her topmasts and lower masts were in one length—pole masts—and her bowsprit and jib boom were also in one piece. She was heavily rigged, her lower yards being 98 feet long and the upper topgallant yards 58 feet in length.

Her various fast speeds, achieved or claimed, while owned by Sir William Garthwaite, will be given as well as the conditions under which they were made, but an average speed of 12½ knots, when loaded, would be considered excellent for her. She was not a handy barque; that could not be expected of a barque of her rig and size. Efforts made to put her round from one tack to another by tacking were rarely successful and she nearly always wore round.

The *Juteopolis* was transferred from her first owners to Mr F E Bliss of

London, who was the manager of the Anglo-American Oil Company, and she was registered under the ownership of this Company in 1900 and put on the trans-Pacific run to carry case oil. In 1911 she was sold to G Windrum and Company of 17 Brunswick Street, Liverpool, for £6,500, and was employed in carrying general and dry bulk cargoes on round the world voyages.

When Mr William Garthwaite bought her she was engaged on a voyage which kept her out of the enemy submarine zone. The voyage had started at Cork on the 21st March, 1917, when she left in ballast for Newport, Mon. She arrived nine days later, loaded for Bahia Blanca, Argentine, and sailed on the 16th May, arriving on the 4th August, 1917. Captain R Parry was her master and William Dempster her first mate. Mr Garthwaite sent his own master and mates out from England to take her over.

Captain Jones, formerly master of the *Centurion*, went out as master, an old man named Chamberlain was her new first mate and Mr J P Williams, of whom we have written in Chapter 5, then 21 years of age, went to join her as second mate. All three sailed in the Royal Mail Steam Packet Company's *Desna* for Buenos Aires before going on to Bahia Blanca, and while there Captain Jones fell sick and was unable to join the barque. Mr Chamberlain, then 70 years of age, was appointed master in place of Captain Jones.

The *Juteopolis* was anchored at Ergineiro White, Bahia Blanca, and when Mr Williams went off in a boat to join her he was surprised by her size. This was his first impression:

> I came up astern [in the boat]. An immense thing she seemed, as indeed she was; one of the largest sailing vessels left in the world then, with her huge lower yards. And looking at her she seemed almost square aloft, being 'bald-headed', the upper topgallant yards appearing, from my angle, almost as long as those beneath. A midship section comprising the crew's quarters, half deck, galley, boiler house etc, was connected with the poop and fo'c'sle by fore and aft bridges. The *Juteopolis* was in ballast, high out of the water,

which made her look even larger than she was and I remember my feeling of pride at being the second mate of so great a ship.

The crew were on board but Captain Parry and Mr Dempster had left her in charge of a young Swede who was her acting second mate. Mr Williams started immediately to prepare the barque for her next passage, which was in ballast to Adelaide.

Captain Chamberlain arrived in Bahia Blanca a week before the *Juteopolis* sailed, and brought a Norwegian with him named Ole Henden who was 49 years of age. He did not have a British certificate, but he was signed on the barque's Articles as first mate at £30 a month on the 25th October. Mr Williams' pay was £14 a month. Mr Williams protested at this, but the *Juteopolis* sailed on the 15th October with the Norwegian as first mate.

The passage was a fine weather one and it took 93 days, the captain keeping the barque to the northward out of the westerly gales. The first mate was over-anxious to pamper and please the men in his watch and often left jobs that should have been done in his watch at night for Mr Williams' watch to do. Sometimes when the second mate relieved the Norwegian first mate and the yards wanted trimming the latter would say: 'Sorry! The wind's only just shifted!'

Mr Williams carried on without saying much until one night he came up on the poop to relieve the first mate at midnight when it was obvious that the barque was carrying too much sail. All sail was set and a heavy squall had hit the barque, and, just as Mr Williams came on to the poop, the fore upper topgallant sail split with a bang and the upper main and mizzen topgallant sails went the same way immediately. Then the barque heeled right over, almost on her beam ends, with the force of the wind in the squall. Fortunately the upper topsails' yards came down the masts when the halliards and topgallant sheets were let go, but it was a near thing to the barque capsizing, or, at the least, being dismasted.

Captain Chamberlain came up on to the poop and the Norwegian first mate tried to put the blame on to young Williams by saying that he himself had gone off watch when the squall struck the barque.

Unfortunately for him his watch were still on deck and the wheel had not been relieved. It was much too obvious to the Captain as to who was responsible. It made trouble between the two mates, which extended to the men in the watches.

The *Juteopolis* arrived at Adelaide on the 16th January, 1918, and there Captain Chamberlain was relieved by Captain Thomas Atkinson, aged 59, of Queenstown, Ireland. He had been sent out by the owners from London and signed the register as master on the 29th January, 1918. Captain Atkinson had been master of the four-masted barque *Eudora*, owned by Thomas Shute of Liverpool. She made several record passages, some when Captain Atkinson commanded her. Her end came when she was sunk by a German submarine, while Captain Atkinson was still her master, 30 miles south-south-west of the Fastnet on the 14th February, 1917. When he came on board the *Juteopolis* he asked Mr Williams a few questions and by them alone the second mate knew instinctively that his new captain was a disciplinarian and that the barque would now be run properly.

Ole Hinden, the first mate, was paid off. While he remained on the barque's Articles the *Juteopolis* could not sail from an Australian port because he did not hold a British certificate. Captain Chamberlain reverted to first mate on the 25th February, 1918. It will be remembered that he was sent out to Bahia Blanca to join the barque as first mate although seventy years of age. It seems obvious that a younger man with the necessary experience was not available. What puzzles the author is why a man of that age, knowing what he was letting himself in for, could offer to go or was persuaded to do so.

The first mate of a windjammer had to be very active. He had to look after himself—the old saying at sea in sailing ships was: 'One hand for the owners and one for yourself'—as well as carry out his duties when standing in the dangerous position at the weather braces. There he had to slack away ropes, on which there was a heavy tension, to trim the yards or wear ship. And that when huge seas were crashing over the weather bulwarks where he was standing. Many quick decisions had to be made which, when put into practice, involved a terrific physical strain. There were many other hazardous jobs which had to be carried out by the officer on watch which could not be evaded. It was certainly not a job for a man of seventy.

During the author's service in square-rigged sailing ships the first mates were mostly young men around twenty-five years of agc. It will be seen how this average age increased in the last years of the British windjammers. It also applied, to a lesser degree, to second mates. There it will be seen that senior apprentices, and those who had just completed their time, were promoted to second mate to a greater extent than was the case ten years previously. Further, one of the best seamen in the fo'c'sle, although he had no certificate, was sometimes signed on as bosun and took charge of a watch as second mate, living aft with the captain and first mate. Some, like 'Dutchy' Voss, made successful officers; but many, although good seamen, were unable to keep discipline and carry out the duties of the officer in charge of the watch. As a matter of interest and importance the author has given correct ages where possible; but they have been taken from official documents and the older men, to the author's knowledge sometimes gave a younger age when signing on.

While loading bags of flour in Adelaide, a small Australian coaster, the *Ready*, came alongside the *Juteopolis* to contribute her quota, and her first mate asked Mr Williams to come on board his steamer for morning tea. He had never heard of morning tea in a ship before so was, to say the least, surprised when he was taken down into the steamer's saloon and there had tea, biscuits and butter—cream crackers, not the windjammers' Liverpool pantiles with weevils. He remarked: 'the absolute luxury of it took me flat aback. I knew then that the streets [of Australia] must indeed be paved with gold; and forty odd years hasn't proved me wrong.'

Mr Williams had a wonderful time in Adelaide; such hospitality he had never known. He was invited to parties to join in crab suppers on the beach, where there was singing to the accompaniment of mouth organs till after midnight, with just enough beer to keep things going and give one a good night's sleep.

The barque loaded a full cargo of about 4,300 tons of flour for New York at £8 a ton, which was a good freight for a windjammer in those days. The *Juteopolis* had been nearly two months in Adelaide when she sailed on the 11th March, 1918. When she left the wharf there was a good crowd of friends to wish them a sorrowful farewell. Three of the crew could hardly be blamed for jumping overboard to swim ashore. But the police boat was there and they were fished out promptly and returned to the barque.

The *Juteopolis* sailed down the St Vincent Gulf, and through Backstairs Passage, to the eastward of Kangaroo Island, on a bright, sunny, fresh morning. Then a course was set for Cape Horn where a wintertime rounding was not looked forward to. Captain Atkinson took the barque well to the southward to cross the South Pacific and a good average speed was made until Cape Horn was approached; then, to the disgust of all on board, the wind went round to blow from the eastward, and continued from that direction day after day. This was a dead muzzler to the barque and meant that the crew had to wear ship in their attempts to round the 'Horn' and reach the South Atlantic. They sailed south to the verge of the pack ice in the short hours of daylight with dawn at eleven in the morning and dark by two in the afternoon. Then with the order 'wear ship', the barque was put about and head-reached to the north. One day Cape Horn was sighted but the wind headed them and they had to 'wear' again and head-reach, with yards braced sharp up on the port tack, to the southward. When well south, they wore again. This time on the end of the northward run the Diego Ramirez was sighted. They had lost ground and were now to the westward of Cape Horn.

This was unusual bad luck, particularly for Captain Atkinson's first passage in the *Juteopolis*. He must have been very disappointed. His second mate gave a brief description of him during those anxious weeks:

'I can see him now. Wearing a long oilskin coat, sou'wester and thigh sea boots; immovable near the wheel on the weather side and giving orders in a strong voice. No complaint, no reference to the bitter cold, and how cold it was! He just stood there and conned the ship.'

Head gales when ships are rounding the 'Horn' from west to east are unusual; but easterly winds and gales do occur although they do not last for so long a period as the westerly gales.

When at last the barque rounded and had run north into the trade winds, they too were disappointing. There was no strength in them and the heavy barque just dragged herself along. And the doldrums, north of the equator, were worse than usual, they brought catspaws of wind from every direction a dozen times a day, and waterspouts too. The passage was long, food was getting short and fish were hard to catch when they were seen. The flour in the holds had to be used.

The tropics were hell. The sails flapped and banged on the masts in the calms; a most unwelcome and annoying noise. The weather was stinking hot and humid and the yards were hauled round from tack to tack in unsuccessful attempts to catch a transient puff of wind. And then came the day when the last of the cabin food was whacked out to all hands. The Official Log Book gave brief details. On one day it recorded that condensed milk and tinned meat were finished and salt meat was cut down to a quarter of a pound a day per man. This occurred in latitude 25° 36′ north, longitude 56° 40′ west.

Then, a piece of good luck at last. On the 7th August, 1918, in latitude 31° 4′ north, longitude 66° 24′ west in a dead calm, a steamer was sighted. Up went the two flag distress signal NC and the steamer altered course to bear down on the *Juteopolis*. She was the Swedish SS *Siluan*. Mr Williams was sent in charge of one of the boats to get what provisions the captain of the steamer could spare. His orders from Captain Atkinson were:

> Give my compliments to the master and tell him how we are placed, and here is a note for him about payment for anything he can let us have. And be sure to get her longitude to check our position.

It should be explained that the correct latitude could be obtained from the meridian altitude of the sun, but the exact working out of the longitude relied on the Greenwich time supplied by the chronometer on board which was corrected in windjammers by a daily rate of gaining or losing. This rate could, and did, change over the long period of a windjammer's passage at sea. Steamers could get their exact Greenwich time every day by wireless and so ensure the working out of a correct longitude.

When Mr Williams boarded the *Siluan* he was given a great welcome, as always happened when a windjammer man went on board a steamship. He was shown up to the captain's cabin while the provisions that could be spared were got together and passed down into the boat. Mr Williams was pressed to have a drink. And then: 'Have another, mister, the boat won't be loaded up yet.' Then the chief officer and the chief engineer insisted that he had a drink with them. When he did get back to the boat he found that he'd had quite enough to drink. He arrived back on board safely with the valuable provisions, but found that he had a job to walk aft to where Captain Atkinson was standing.

'What is her longitude?' the captain asked. Mr Williams had forgotten to ask for it and replied: 'I don't know sir.' The Captain gave a dim smile, the first time he had smiled for weeks, and said in a surprisingly gentle voice: 'Have a lie-down for a bit, mister!'

He did so and when the drink had worn off he came on deck again feeling more ashamed of himself than he has ever felt since. When he saw his captain he apologised. 'Don't worry about it, my boy, all of us make fools of ourselves at times!' Captain Atkinson replied.

Mr Williams said that, curiously enough, it made a big change in their relationship. When things were quiet the Captain would come up on the poop and talk to him about the ships that he had been in and of his life at sea. He was married and master of a windjammer when only twenty-two years of age, and of all the years he had been at sea he had only spent a total of two with his wife who was then dead. He was born in Cork, the son of a British naval captain stationed there, and was a Protestant living in a Roman Catholic community. Deeply religious, stern of character, his barque or ship and his duty to her owners were his whole life. Mr Williams, the young second mate, and his old captain became friends in a detached but warm way, and he admired him immensely the whole time he served under him.

The captain of the *Siluan* sent the *Juteopolis* 50 lbs of salt beef, 100 lbs of salt pork and two bags of potatoes which were divided equally among the captain, and the crew, including, of course, the two mates.

After the steamer left the *Juteopolis* the barque experienced better luck and fair winds took them to the east coast of the United States, where

Captain Atkinson expected to raise Fire Island Light in latitude 4° 38′ north, longitude 70° 13′ west; but no sign of it was seen. Visibility became bad and the barque was stood away from the land under easy sail until daylight. At dawn the *Juteopolis* was headed again for the land which was sighted at three o'clock that afternoon. Captain Atkinson would not take a waiting tug until her master dropped his price for towing.

The *Juteopolis* was towed into Eyrie Basin on the 18th August, 1918, and moored there in company with several others of the last of the British windjammers. John Stewart's *Falkirk* was there with the *Celtic Glen* and the *Hilston.* The pilot told the captain that there was an epidemic of sickness ashore and 'people were dying like flies'. All the hospitals were full. After going ashore Captain Atkinson confirmed this. 'Its the Pneumonic 'Flu' he told Mr Williams. It was, in fact, what was known then as the Spanish 'Flu.

Most of the crew went ashore and were paid off. A few remained in the ship. On the morning of the 21st September, 1918, when Mr Williams went into the fo'c'sle to turn the men to, to start the day's work, he found a Swedish seaman, aged 23, named Oscar Mellin, dead in his bunk, a victim of the 'flu.

Soon after the barque's arrival, a friend of the captain came on board to lunch. Mr Williams went along the wharf to meet him and escort him on board. They were walking along the after deck to the poop when the visitor staggered and fell. Captain Atkinson came down the poop ladder to help Mr Williams get the visitor on to his feet when the latter gave a few gasps and died. Later the police came on board to report that many of the crew had died on shore.

It was at this time, August 1918, that young Pearce joined the *Juteopolis* as a first voyage apprentice. He is now Captain F W J Pearce of Devon, retired Peninsular and Oriental Line Commander. Seven other apprentices joined the barque with him, there being two older apprentices serving on board as well as two ordinary seamen. Thirteen apprentices and seamen were taken ashore to hospital suffering from Spanish 'Flu, of which three apprentices died.

The Official Log records that the following apprentices died in hospital:

Robert Roy King, aged 16, of Northwich, Cheshire, on the 24th September, 1918; Francis Henry Drake Ridd, aged 17, of Exeter, Devon, on the 25th September; and Humphrey Jones, aged 17, of Llandrillo, North Wales, on the 26th September.

It is strange that in the midst of all this sickness and death, Mr Williams should remember that it was while at New York, on this occasion, that he saw, for the first time, milk for sale in a bottle. Condensed milk was always used in windjammers. A milkman came on board and he bought a bottle which he noticed was thin with cream on top. This he put on his plate of breakfast burgoo (porridge made with water) and it was one of the most delicious meals he had ever tasted. In his opinion the food in windjammers was so bad that taste meant nothing on a long passage; it filled one's stomach and that was all.

Mr Chamberlain, the old first mate, had a habit, when Captain Atkinson first joined the ship in Adelaide, of lingering at the saloon table over his meals. One day, the captain looked at him fairly straight and said in his grim tone: 'Mister, you've been here too long, slow at meals, slow at work; it's time you were on deck!' After hearing that, Mr Williams used to rush through his meals and get out on deck. He confessed that he still retains the habit although it affected his digestion for years after.

Captain Henry was master of the *Celtic Glen*, afterwards the *Garthforce*, which was then moored near the *Juteopolis*. Mr Williams could not speak highly enough of him and his wife. While in New York Captain Henry came on board to give Mr Williams two weeks' pay owed from the time he served on board the captain's ship some years before.

Mr Chamberlain was paid off at New York on the 23rd September, 1918, after a bout of sickness and Mr Williams took his place as first mate at £25 a month. Mr A O Zrinyi, aged 46, who came from the *Celtic Glen*, was signed on the *Juteopolis* as second mate. He was a naturalised British subject, holding a British second mate's certificate, whose home was at Church Stretton, Shropshire.

Captain Price, who was the marine superintendent for the Marine Navigation Company (W Garthwaite) in New York, came on board to interview Mr Williams: 'The captain speaks well of you,' he said, 'do you want the first mate's job?' 'Yes sir,' Williams replied, 'but I have only a second mate's certificate.'

'I know that,' Captain Price said. 'But I've arranged for you to go to Halifax, Nova Scotia, where there is an examination being held next week, and the bargain is that you go there and if you pass we will pay the fare and you can have the job. If you don't pass you can pay the fare and come back to your ship as second mate. What about it?'

Naturally Mr Williams agreed and went to Halifax at once and fixed himself up with lodgings. He took his letter of introduction to the Company's Agent and on the next day attended the navigation school to start his studies. Then came the first set-back. He was told that the examination had started that morning. With the Agent's help he got admitted, although at first the examiner held him up because he hadn't renewed his first aid certificate. But the Agent won over this objection and Mr Williams sat down to do the navigation paper. When he had finished it, and took it up to the examiner, the latter pointed out that the answer for the 'Sumner'—a lengthy but not difficult problem in navigation—was wrong. He was allowed to take it back to his desk and check it. He got the same result again. It appeared that the examiner had got hold of the wrong set of answers, but the young lady secretary found the right ones and Mr Williams got through the first day. He was lucky with the rest of the examinations and wrote or gave the correct answers. The number of his Provisional First Mate's Certificate, obtained in Halifax, Nova Scotia, was 043550. The certificate was Provisional because Mr Williams had not served the necessary period as second mate to allow him to obtain the full certificate, but as soon as the balance of that period was served his certificate would automatically become a full first mate's certificate, which it did. In the meantime he was qualified to serve as first mate.

The *Juteopolis* loaded a general cargo in New York which included silk stockings and women's dresses, goods which were attractive to anyone inclined to pilfering cargoes. It certainly was an unusual cargo for a windjammer. One morning Captain Atkinson came on board and told Mr Williams that he had been offered the crew of the four-masted barque *Alice A Leigh.* They were in prison for refusing duty on board their barque and the prison authorities wanted to get rid of them. They signed on the Articles of the *Juteopolis*, a mixed lot, including seamen from Britain, America, Scandinavia and other countries. They proved a bad lot and Captain Atkinson's orders to his two mates was to keep them working without a break during their duty time on deck.

An early episode was when a young Russian Finn raised his hand to hit Mr Zrinyi who was only half the size of the Finn. As quick as lightning the second mate whipped a belaying pin out of the main fife rail, and, before the Finn could strike, he floored him to the deck with one blow. Captain Atkinson and Mr Williams ran down off the poop to the assistance of Mr Zrinyi, but there was no need. He stood there cursing his watch and offering to flatten any one of them who would step forward. There were no takers and Mr Zrinyi had no more trouble with his watch. This was the method adopted with troublesome men in windjammers in the author's day. It was always successful and the men accepted it as the acknowledged method of keeping discipline.

The Articles of Agreement signed by the crew were dated the 16th October, 1918, and the owners were given as The Marine Navigation Company, 5 Lloyds Avenue, London EC. The port of registry of the *Juteopolis* was given as Liverpool.

When the barque's loading was completed she was towed down the Hudson River on the 1st November, 1918, a bitterly cold, blustery day. Much to Captain Atkinson's annoyance he received orders from the Admiralty to sail within a hundred miles of the Atlantic seaboard, instead of making well out to the eastward. This placed the barque too far to the westward to make an easy rounding of Cape San Roque, the north-east point of Brazil. The west-setting Equatorial Current and the south-east trade winds made it more difficult to keep clear of the coast of Brazil. In the event it took the barque 62 days to get down to the southward of Cape San Roque. The big heavy yards were hauled round day and night to a continually shifting light wind and eventually the barque had to make to the northward to get sufficient easting.

She arrived at Sydney on the 17th March, 1919, after a long passage of 136 days, which, but for the Admiralty routing, could have been an excellent fast passage. The tug *Champion* took the *Juteopolis* in tow outside Sydney Heads and she was moored at Wooloomooloo, just below the Botanical Gardens. It was learned then that the war had finished over four months ago.

The troublesome crew were paid off and peace reigned on board for a period. One day when Mr Williams and Captain Atkinson were going ashore through the Botanical Gardens to the Agent's office, a young girl approached the Captain and said: 'Give us a shilling, Captain?' 'Why do you call me Captain?' he asked. 'Captain!' she replied. 'All the rain in heaven couldn't wash the salt out of your face!'

'How right she was,' Mr Williams said. 'She got her shilling and one from me as well.'

When the cargo was discharged the *Champion* towed the *Juteopolis* northward to Newcastle where a cargo of coal was loaded for Valparaiso for orders. The usual hospitality was enjoyed at the Stockton Mission to Seamen.

The barque arrived at Valparaiso on the 25th July, 1919, and left three days later for Carrizal Bajo, Chile, where she arrived on the 17th August. The coals were consigned to a copper mine, and before discharging could be started, the barque had to be moved further inshore to a small bay which seemed to have been cut vertically out of the cliffs which towered hundreds of feet above. There were no tugs there so the barque's boats were put over the side and the two lifeboats and two gigs were fully manned and succeeded in towing the *Juteopolis* some two or three miles inshore. All hands, except the Captain, the cook, and one or two of the men who were not so strong, were rowing in the boats. She was a heavy barque loaded with 4,300 tons of coal. As soon as the off-shore wind died down in the early morning, the tow started. It can be said with certainty that she was the last big British windjammer to be towed by her own boats.

Here, it will be remembered, Mr Williams left the *Juteopolis* on the 21st August, 1919, to join the *Wray Castle* at Caleta Buena as first mate and Mr Zrinyi was promoted to first mate of the *Juteopolis* at a wage of £25 a month.

On the morning that Mr Williams left the barque he had to go up the cliffs in the rail car to the 'Alto' to pick up the Longitudinal Railway on the plains beyond the mountains. He stood at the top of the cliffs, 2,000 feet above the Bay, and looked down on the *Juteopolis*. She looked a tiny perfect model of a four-masted barque in a deep blue setting and every detail stood out clearly from the height at which he gazed down upon her. This was the last he was to see of the barque he had served in as second and first mate for twenty-two months. It was a sad parting.

A young seaman who served in the fo'c'sle of the *Juteopolis* when she was the *Garthpool*, some time after Mr Williams had left her, had picked up and taken one of her Mate's Log Books. Later, after the young seaman had passed his examinations for master, he joined one of the steamships of the Federal Line as fourth officer. His captain was an old shipmate of Mr Williams when they both served in windjammers. When the captain learnt that his fourth officer had an old log book of the *Garthpool*, he asked him who the first mate was who wrote it up. 'Someone named Williams,' was the reply. And so the log book returned to the first mate who wrote it and sometimes he reads it and thinks back on that life of so many years ago, now vanished for ever; and of Captain Atkinson and Mr Zrinyi, and the men and boys of the *Juteopolis*, the last British windjammer.

The *Juteopolis* discharged part of her cargo at Carrizal Bajo and sailed northward to Iquique to complete the unloading. Nitrate was then loaded for Durban. She arrived off Durban at midnight on Christmas Eve, 1919, and hove-to waiting for a tug and a pilot to take her into the port. Imagine the disappointment of everyone on board when they did not come and the barque was swept to the southward by the Agulhas Current. She did not reach the entrance to Durban again until the 9th January, 1920, when she was towed in and moored at the quay.

After the nitrate was discharged, coal was loaded for Bunbury, Western Australia, and there the voyage ended and the crew were paid off. The new voyage started on the 12th May, 1920, and Mr John Collins, aged 58, was signed on as first mate. He had been master of several sailing ships before becoming a pilot at Newcastle, New South Wales. He left the pilotage to join the *Juteopolis*. There may be some significance in this in view of what happened later on the passage home. Mr W M Thomson of

Liverpool, aged 21, had been promoted to third mate on the 11th April, 1921.

The *Juteopolis* left Bunbury on the 30th May, 1920, for Durban, loaded with a cargo of jarrah wood sleepers. She arrived on the 12th July, 1920, and loaded coals there for Port Louis, Mauritius, but when the big Port tug came to tow her to sea, her engines were put the wrong way and she cut into the side of the barque with her stem. Part of the coals was unloaded and the barque was listed over for temporary repairs. Then the remainder of the coals was discharged and the *Juteopolis* went into dry dock to be permanently repaired. Rock ballast was taken in by the crew and the barque sailed for Bunbury, arriving on Christmas Day, 1920, just in time for the start of a two months' railway strike.

A new Official Log Book was started in Bunbury on the 1st March, 1921, and the name of the barque was entered in it as the *Garthpool*. The owners were listed as 'The Marine Navigation Company Limited, 5 Lloyds Avenue, London EC, and the port of registry was given as Liverpool. The crew were deemed to be complete with twenty-eight, not less than seventeen being sailors.

The *Garthpool* left Bunbury loaded once again with jarrah wood sleepers on the 12th March, 1921, for Cape Town, arriving on the 21st April. Here Mr William Wylie, aged 34, of London, joined the barque on the 12th May, 1921 as second mate.

The next passage was made in ballast to Port Adelaide where the barque arrived on the 17th August. Her orders were to load with wheat at Port Lincoln, in the Spencer Gulf for Falmouth and she arrived to load on the 31st August, 1921. When she sailed on the 25th October, Captain Atkinson decided to take the westward route across the Great Australian Bight and round the Cape of Good Hope.

On the way home Captain Atkinson was taken ill. The first intimation was entered in the Official Log Book:

> 30th November, 1921 at 8.10 am in latitude 23° 15′ south, longitude 84° 16′ east.
>
> Captain Atkinson has been taken ill, the illness being a kind of

stroke which left him in a semi-conscious state, the use of the right arm and leg being partially lost, or nearly paralysed. We assisted him with difficulty from the charthouse to his cabin and laid him on the bed, our efforts being directed to give him rest and to restore full consciousness in which we were only partly successful. The Captain had lost the power of speech but understood in part at least, what we were trying to do for him, and tried to assist with his left arm and following movements with his eyes.

(signed) John Collins, Commanding Officer.
Wiliam Wylie, Acting first mate.
William Thomson, acting second mate.

1st December, 1921. Noon position, latitude 22° 48′ south, longitude 82° 17′ east. am and pm.
The captain slept very well through the night but not answering when spoken to when awake. A close watch [was] kept during [the] night and day, either by third mate Thomson, or one of the older apprentices, the officer of the watch also paying frequent visits. With regard to medicine he had brought a stock specially prepared by the doctor who attended him at Port Adelaide and [it was] regularly administered by the steward. William Thomson, the third mate, had been in particular attendance on the captain for some years [and] also at the hospital in Port Adelaide.

4th December, 1921. latitude 22° 13′ south, longitude 75° 24′ east. Noon:
During the last three days the Captain was about the same. He took his medicine regularly and took food—mostly chicken broth, beef tea, arrowroot and canned pears. His temperature [is] nearly normal. His pulse varying from 65 to 75 beats per minute but respiration from 23 to 27 per minute. We wash his body morning and evening and spray the skin with spirit.
10 pm latitude 22° 3′ south, longitude 75° 24′ east. This night the Captain appears to be getting worse, the respiration being much quicker, but [the] temperature still normal.

8 am 5th December, 1921, latitude 22° 3′ south, longitude at noon, 73° 26′ east.
This morning the Captain was much worse, respiration being very rapid [54] and pulse very irregular. He took his medicine but little nourishment in the morning.
2.25 pm latitude 22° 4′ south, longitude 73° 18′ east.
At 2.25 pm the Captain died in the presence of Mr Wylie, Mr Thomson, E Baines, apprentice, and myself, John Collins. For half an hour before this he had great effort in breathing. Inhaling treatment gave him no relief [and] it was evident he was dying. After two great gasps for breath he passed away without regaining [the] power of speech.
At 6.30 pm all hands were permitted to take a last look as an act of respect to our late Commander's remains.

8 am 6th December, 1921, latitude 22° 6′ south, longitude 71° 22′ east.
At 8 am we buried the remains of our late Captain, all hands being mustered to attend the burial. The flag [ensign] hoisted [at] half mast and an ensign spread over the bier. I then read out the service for the burial of the dead at sea, and the body shrouded in canvas, and heavily weighted, was committed to the deep. All hands repeated the Lord's Prayer and then dispersed, this sad ceremony being over. The weather being hot and sultry the body had begun to smell, hence the necessity of a speedy burial.

(Signed) John Collins, Commanding Officer.
William Wylie, Second mate (Acting first mate).
William Thomson, Acting second mate.

Apprentice F W J Pearce was promoted to third mate.
The *Garthpool* reached Falmouth on the 5th March, 1922 and received orders to proceed to Sunderland to discharge her cargo.

The *Garthpool*

The *Garthpool* left Falmouth for Sunderland in tow of the tug *Homer* at 6 pm on the 8th March, 1922. At 3.30 am on the 9th March, when she was approximately fifteen miles west-south-west of Start Point, the tug's crew let go the towing hawser in a severe storm and the tug was soon lost to sight astern. Half an hour later the two lower topsails, which were the only sails set on the barque, blew away. This was followed by other sails, already made fast on the yards, blowing out of the gaskets that held them and being torn to ribbons. The fore and main braces and the lifts on the yards carried away, and the yards, which were swinging dangerously, were secured temporarily with great difficulty. The cross seas were incredibly high and the decks were swept with heavy seas fore and aft, gear carrying away through the heavy rolling and the hurricane force wind. The barque was in a helpless condition and at 2 pm the Captain had the distress signal, NC, hoisted.

This storm is known as 'the famous storm of March, 1922', when a wind force of 108 miles per hour was recorded at Scilly, the highest recorded in England at that time.

At 2.30 pm that afternoon, the 9th March, the ss *Thermisto*, a Dutch steamer, approached the *Garthpool* and agreed to tow her to Portland. The tow rope was connected at the third attempt but it was 7.30 pm before this was accomplished. At 8 pm it was blowing a north-west gale and a French Light was in sight; but it was not until midnight that the steamer was able to make headway, and then the tow rope parted. The steamer stood by the barque till daylight when another tow rope was put on board. By this time the weather had moderated and the *Thermisto* towed the *Garthpool* to Portland where she arrived at 1.15 pm on the 10th March, a local tug being engaged to tow the barque into the harbour where she anchored with two anchors down.

New sails were bent on the yards, repairs were carried out, and then on the 18th March the *Garthpool* set out again for Sunderland in tow of two tugs. Off the Sunk Lighthouse she encountered a northerly gale with a blizzard and the tow rope of one of the tugs parted. The other tug turned the *Garthpool* to the southward and towed her to an anchorage in the Downs where she rode out the bad weather. She reached Sunderland on the 26th March, 1922; the crew were paid off and the apprentices went home on leave.

The *Garthpool* discharged her cargo in the South Dock and then shifted to the North Dock to lay up. On the 11th January, 1923, she was towed to Tollesbury on the River Blackwater in Essex to lay up. She arrived there on the 13th January. According to the Coastal Articles for this short passage Captain P Owens was her master and her owners were recorded as The Marine Navigation Company of Canada, 12 Board Buildings, 42 Sacramont Street, Montreal, Canada. Mr J H Craig was her second mate. He held a second mate's foreign-going certificate, and on board with him were eight able seamen, three apprentices and a cook. The eight able seamen were employed for the run only and were glad to get the job. They all held master mariner's certificates. It was the time of the bad shipping slump when master mariners were selling matches in Oxford Street, London, in an effort to keep their families from starving. One was lucky enough to get a job washing up in a London restaurant. Many had to sell up their homes to buy food. And this a few years after the First World War when the Merchant Navy lost such a large percentage of masters, officers and seamen at sea from enemy action in their persistent efforts to bring food to the very people that were now denying it to them. How ungrateful can a nation be? At least one of the last of the British windjammers provided a few meals for their families.

Mr Craig remained on board the *Garthpool* at Tollesbury as shipkeeper. She remained there until the 16th August, 1924, and then was towed to Dunkirk. According to the Home Trade Articles for that passage Captain David Roberts was her master, Mr William Wylie her first mate and Mr J H Craig her second mate. The apprentices on board were Rolfe, Herbert, Kent, Simpson, Martin, Gray, Adams and J D L Williams. All except the latter had served in other windjammers of the Company. Mr Craig's young brother, G A Craig, was the deck boy.

The author must interpose here to mention that neither Captain J H Craig, as he is at the time of writing, nor Captain J D L Williams, now Regional Controller of the Department of Shipping and Transport, Tasmania, can remember Captains Owens or Roberts on board the

Garthpool during this period; but Captain Craig has written to the author mentioning that Captain David Roberts was the last master before he joined the *Garthpool* and that Captain Roberts had left a sea chest containing his navigation and seamanship books with a note that he would not require them any more. Captain Craig still has the volume of 'Lecky's Wrinkles' that was in the chest. With regard to Captain Craig, he had served in Garthwaite's barques *Invercauld* and *Inversnaid* and had been an officer in one of the Company's steamers. He had joined the *Garthpool* as shipkeeper while she was in Sunderland. Captain Wylie, aged 37, from Wanstead, Essex, joined her as master at Tollesbury, took her across to Dunkirk, and sailed in her as master on the next voyage. His salary was £30 a month. The voyage started at Dunkirk on the 19th August, 1924.

The *Garthpool* went into dry dock at Dunkirk and her port of registry on her stern was clearly 'Montreal'. She wore the Canadian Merchant Navy flag. Mr Murdoch Macdonald, aged 49, was her first mate. He was a Glasgow man and held a first mate's certificate. The Captain and the two mates served in their respective capacities for the voyage and left the barque in Birkenhead on the 13th September, 1926.

The apprentices were experienced and capable seamen; far more useful on board than the majority of the able seamen that could be obtained at that time in spite of the shipping slump. Twelve seamen were carried in the fo'c'sle, but although some were efficient, some were poor, desperate wretches either destitute or with some reason for wishing to get away from England for a long period. There were also two lads from one of the training establishments on the River Thames—not HMS *Worcester*—who were put in the half deck with the apprentices.

Young Williams, not to be confused with Captain Sir John Prothero Williams, was making his first voyage at sea. He had joined the *Garthpool* at Tollesbury as an apprentice from HMS *Worcester*, the cadet ship on the Thames, in the summer of 1924, to serve a three years' apprenticeship. He first met Captain Wylie when the ship was being towed out of the Blackwater River and had a shock. The captain hailed him when he was working on the after deck, with 'Hey, you!' and the young apprentice turned to see his captain crouched over the rail at the forward end of the poop wearing a dirty serge suit, a flannel shirt held at the throat by a cheap brass stud and a trilby hat pulled over his ears. He was unshaven and glaring; not a bit like a *Worcester* cadet's idea of a ship's captain. But he was Williams' captain and he sprang to attention and saluted him.

'Tell the mate!' the captain growled.

'Tell him what, sir?' the young apprentice asked him respectfully.

'Tell the bloody bastard I want him!' the captain shouted back.

'My education had begun,' Captain Williams told me.

'I ran forward to where the mate and two of the seamen were swearing and cursing at the tow rope, and translated the message as: 'The Captain's compliments, sir, and would you please speak to him!' The first mate was a kindly man but what he had to say when he recovered from his astonishment at being wanted aft at a time when he was involved critically with getting the tow rope fast, advanced young William's education further.

Williams was in the first mate's watch for the whole of the voyage and found him placid and tolerant although an experienced and able officer. If he had a fault it was his liking for a drink. Mr Martin, the third mate, was also in the first mate's watch. He was still serving his apprenticeship and was young. He was smart, energetic, efficient and a strict disciplinarian. One of the seamen, resenting his disciplinary methods, let go the halliards holding a bosun's chair in which he was sitting aloft. He crashed to the deck, was badly injured, and had to be taken to hospital. He was left behind when the barque sailed. But he recovered and joined the *Garthpool* on her next voyage as second mate. Those windjammer lads were tough. Simpson, the senior apprentice, served as third mate for this voyage.

When the *Garthpool* sailed from Dunkirk on the 19th August for Campbellton, New Brunswick, Canada, Captain Wylie set course down the English Channel, but, after beating against a south-westerly gale without making any progress, decided to sail round the north of Scotland. The passage took forty days, the barque arriving at Campbellton on the 28th September. Westerly gales were experienced and the day's runs varied from 48 to 310 nautical miles.

The barque towed up the Restigouche River to load timber at

Dalhousie. She created a record there, for 1,200 standards of timber were loaded into her in ten days using her steam winches. Lionel Adams, the apprentice, now Chairman of the Australian Canned Fruits Board, Melbourne, was the donkeyman (donkey boiler and winch operator). He claimed that this job enabled him to dodge the hard work on board. The author would have thought that to look after the boiler and the steam winches at the hatchways would have been enough work for anyone.

Part of the cargo was stowed on the fore and after decks, filling them completely to the tops of the bulwarks. A single life line was rigged along the top of the timber, which was used as a deck, on each side of the barque. Temporary leads were made for the running gear for working the yards and sails, and there were plenty of traps for the feet along the top of the timber. The whole set-up was particularly bad on dark nights, especially as no lighting was used on deck in windjammers. The hazards were obviously greater in bad weather when heavy seas were breaking over the timber. It was extraordinary that no one was washed overboard; there were several narrow escapes.

The *Garthpool* sailed on the 5th November for Adelaide and Melbourne taking 101 days to Port Adelaide where she arrived on the 14th February, 1925. When part of the cargo had been discharged the barque sailed through Backstairs Passage round the coast to Melbourne in eight days to unload the remainder. This short passage was hazardous. The barque was first held up with head winds, and anchored for three days in the Gulf of St Vincent. She was near the Trowbridge Shoal Reef, only 30 miles from Port Adelaide, when a heavy squall, with lightning and thunder, was experienced. In trying to clear the edge of the shoal the vessel had to be brought into the wind and the anchor let go quickly while the barque still had all sail set. Many of the sails were split and lost. On the next day the barque was sailed to a safe anchorage and the lost sails were replaced. Captain Wylie said it was a case of either losing the barque or the sails as she very nearly ran on to the reef. After this the *Garthpool* sailed through the Backstairs Passage and excellent time was made from Cape Otway to Gellibrand Lighthouse in 9 hours 15 minutes. Melbourne was reached on the 11th March.

It was intended that the *Garthpool* should load grain for the United Kingdom, but there were no cargoes available and she lay at anchor in Hobson's Bay for four months. Some of the crew were paid off and others deserted. Those of the apprentices who had completed their Indentures asked Captain Wylie to release them so that they could take their examinations for second mate. He refused, pointing out a clause in the Indentures which required them, if their apprenticeships finished during the voyage, to sign on the barque's Articles as able seamen at a small rate of pay. This was in the author's Indentures and was common to most windjammer apprentices although some captains did release their apprentices in ports abroad.

Captain Wylie was adamant and some of the time-expired apprentices on board left the barque one night and did not return. This could have been serious, for without their endorsed Indentures and a character reference they would have been unable to sit for their second mate's examination. When the late Captain John King Davis, the Antarctic explorer, who was then Director of Navigation at Melbourne, heard of this he persuaded Captain Wylie to surrender the Indentures to the apprentices concerned, endorsed as completed, and provide testimonials of character. I believe there was a refusal to clear the ship for leaving the port until this was done. Whether this was so, or not, we do know that the Indentures were surrendered to their ex-apprentice owners.

The two boys from the sail training establishments on the Thames deserted here. There was a curious story told about one of them. He joined a homeward-bound cargo liner as a mess boy, and, getting himself into some trouble, leapt overboard off Cape Guardafui, in Africa, at the entrance to the Gulf of Aden, with the intention of swimming ashore. He took a red ensign with him to impress the natives. One of the crew, whom he had taken into his confidence, informed the officer on watch, and although the liner was stopped and turned round to go to his assistance, the lad was never found.

After the long stay in Hobson's Bay the *Garthpool* loaded grain at Geelong for Callao, Peru, and left about the 19th July. Several young Australians joined here and were accommodated in the halfdeck. They had no intention of taking up the sea as a profession, but were out for the adventure of the voyage. They learnt their duties quickly and were useful hands. The new crew in the fo'c'sle, who were mostly Australian seamen from coastal vessels, were very discontented with the food and conditions of working on board, and showed it.

The *Garthpool* sailed to the eastward, passing about 230 miles to the northward of New Zealand and on the tenth day out was in latitude 33° 15′ south, longitude 180°. She was then steered to the southward until latitude 48° 40′ south, longitude 170° west was reached. The furthest south reached on this passage was latitude 50° 30′ in longitude 152° west. Captain Wylie then made to the northward. When in latitude 45° south a head wind was encountered for nine days and he then took his barque down to 49° south. Such alterations in course I feel were unusual on this passage and the author can offer no reason for them.

The passage time from Geelong to Callao was about 78 days, a long passage. After the grain cargo had been discharged, and the ballast stowed in the bottom of the main hold, the barque sailed for Sydney on the 23rd November, 1925. Some of the crew had deserted in Callao and could not be replaced. The only man who joined the ship was put on board as a 'Distressed British Seaman'. He was a half-witted beachcomber, known as Paddy the Bum, eaten up with syphilis and had no nose or roof to his mouth. He wandered unhappily round the decks, no help at all, just an awful warning. But he was a shipmate, however undesirable, and there can be no doubt that conditions were made as comfortable on board for him as was possible.

The passage to Sydney was made in the fine weather of the south-east trade winds, the *Garthpool* arriving on the 7th January, 1926, after a passage of 45 days. On fine weather passages in the old windjammers gramophones were played in the second dog-watch, and on occasions in the *Garthpool*, Captain Wylie lent his records to the apprentices.

After leaving Callao a course was set to the westward for about 20 days to a position in latitude 11° 20′ south, longitude 139° 10′ west, fifty miles south of the Marquesas. Then the barque passed 160 miles to the northward of Makatea, Society Islands, and 270 miles north of Tahiti.

On the 4th January Lord Howe Island was sighted; the only land seen when passing through the lovely island-studded seas of the South Pacific.

The 180th meridian, the date line, was crossed at midnight on the 24th December, and the next day should have been the 26th December to conform with the International Date which demanded the time to be advanced by twenty-four hours. There were only two official holidays on board the windjammers, Good Friday and Christmas Day. As far as the crew of the *Garthpool* were concerned there should have been no Christmas Day, 1925, but Captain Wylie decided it should be celebrated on the 26th December.

In Sydney, a full cargo of grain, 56,000 bags, was loaded at No 8 Pyremont for Falmouth for orders. While moored there some actors and actresses came on board on Sunday 14th February, 1926, to take part in a film. The crew signed on for the passage home on the 16th February and at 6 am the next day the *Garthpool* was towed to an anchorage. Senior apprentice Rolfe was promoted to third mate that day and moved to his cabin aft, off the saloon.

On the 1st March two tugs came alongside the barque at 5.30 am and the anchor cable was hove-up with steam from the donkey boiler working the capstan. By 8 am the *Garthpool* had cleared Sydney Heads and two hours later all sail was set. The pilot left at 11 am.

The wind was from the south-east, a head wind, so the new hands were soon at work hauling the yards round to put the barque on opposing tacks as required. One of them was a genial, tow-haired giant who was taken at first to be Swedish until he opened his mouth. It was then very soon realised that he was a cockney. 'Cock' Sanderson had been a London River lighterman. Even *he* wasn't sure how he had come to be 'on the beach' in Sydney. His only possession for the homeward passage round Cape Horn was a pair of dungaree trousers. He managed to get a flour sack from the steward to make himself a vest, and he used to carry a box of straw aft to stand in to protect his bare feet when he took his trick at the wheel. But he was always cheerful and helpful to everyone on board, and the first to tackle any unpleasant or hazardous job in his watch.

The apprentices admired him tremendously and rigged him out with boots, warm clothes, oilskins and seaboots for Cape Horn as well as supplying him with warm blankets for his bunk.

I have met this type of man at sea in windjammers. They were 'the salt of the earth', the finest shipmates to have on board a square-rigged ship. It is often said that the Scandinavians made the best able seamen in sailing ships. I found German seamen most excellent, and it has already been mentioned that French sailors from Brittany are exceptionally good, but I maintain that Cockney seamen were superior to them all. No sailor could be better and more reliable on a yard when taking in the foresail in a strong gale. There is more to it than that; it is their cheerful disposition and encouraging attitude when things are at their worst on board. The Cockney seamen in ocean-going sailing ships go back to the East Indiamen in the early seventeenth century and follow on in the Blackwall Frigates, the China Tea and the Wool Clippers, and finally, in this century, in the windjammers. This is a tradition that cannot be beaten and it has produced the best seamen in the world.

By Saturday the 6th March the *Garthpool* was down in the Roaring Forties, latitude 40° 54′ south, longitude 159° east, and the weather so deteriorated that the courses (the lower square sails) on the fore, main and mizzen masts, and all the upper topgallant sails had to be taken in and made fast. At 7.30 am on the 10th March the Snares, to the southward of New Zealand, were sighted and the weather moderated. But not for long. The crew were soon making fast again those sails that had been set when the gale eased. By the 16th March the *Garthpool* was down in latitude 50° south and she continued to cross the South Pacific in that latitude.

When soundings were taken at 6 am on the 18th March there was 5½ inches of water in the well which indicated a leak. It was found to come from the transom right aft where some plates had been renewed in Callao. At 8 pm that night the water in the well (amidships) had increased to 7½ inches and there was 13 inches in the bilges aft. There was some difficulty in getting the pumps to suck, but once they were started they were manned every watch; a wearying task made more disagreeable by the vile stench of rotted grain soaked in the water.

On the 22nd March the wind dropped to a calm and for that twenty-four hours only 52 miles were sailed. The following days were as bad, the runs being 45, 37 and 61 miles. In fact the average speed across the South Pacific in latitude 50° was low.

On the 23rd March an albatross was caught, photographed on the poop and then safely launched over the side and no harm was done to the bird. No doubt it was coincidental, but after the albatross was caught the barque met a head wind which lasted for nine days. Worse was to follow. On the 3rd April the weather deteriorated and all hands were furling the crossjack and mainsail in a strong gale and a heavy sea. After they had made the foresail fast at eight o'clock on the next morning all hands were called aft to splice the main brace (have a tot of hot rum). Many of the hard weather sails were split in this gale, had to be unbent and sent down and the reserves sent up in their place.

On Monday the 19th April, 1926, in the morning watch Mount Darwin, 6,800 feet in height, in Tierra del Fuego, was sighted about 75 miles off. The weather was fine and all sail was set. The barque's position at noon that day was latitude 55° 56′ south, longitude 71° 41′ west.

On the next day the Diego Ramirez islets and rocks were passed at 7 am and Cape Horn was abeam at 2.30 pm only two miles away. The barque was then fifty days out from Sydney. Staten Island was passed on the next day but was not in sight; but the east coast of the Falkland Islands was sighted as the barque sailed to the northward.

The pumps had been kept going every watch and on the 26th April the crew started shifting the bags of wheat in the after hatch. In two days' time they got to the bilges and cleaned the stinking grain out of them. That made things easier, but the bad luck was to continue. Was it really caused by that albatross? We have a photographic record of him and he doesn't look a spiteful bird. On Saturday the 1st May, a pin sheared off the steering gear when a big sea was running and the wheel could not be turned to port. The barque broached-to into the trough of the sea and with all hands on deck she was got back on to her course with no more damage done. Then a tackle was rigged to move the rudder to starboard and the wheel was used for moving the rudder to port. The system answered but the steering made possible by it was far from satisfactory and the course was altered for Rio de Janeiro for repairs.

As the ship made to the northward the weather improved. The hold ventilators were uncovered and some of the hatches were taken off for a few hours a day to ventilate the holds. The crew were still pumping and shifting the cargo. Steam was raised in the donkey boiler and an attempt was made to steer the ship with power-driven capstans. It was a failure and, after the sails got aback through the barque falling right off her course, this method was abandoned and steering by tackle and wheel was resumed.

On Thursday the 13th May a tug came out of Rio de Janeiro harbour to tow the *Garthpool* in and she anchored after a 74 days' passage from Sydney. About 30,000 bags of grain were discharged out of the 56,000 on board, and the barque went into dry dock for repairs. Three patches were put on her hull plating and she went back to anchor to reload her wheat.

While in Rio de Janeiro the apprentices were given the opportunity of going ashore and on one not-to-be-forgotten occasion were given week-end leave and thirty dollars to spend. They stayed at the Europe Hotel, went to a theatre to see a show with the title, 'Iron Horse', and on the next day had a tour round the City and saw the wonderful views. They also went to a cinema to see the film 'Johanna'. Altogether they had a most enjoyable time with quite a lot of ship visiting—chiefly for the meals—as well as outings and entertainments arranged by the 'Missions to Seamen'. Captain Wylie could hardly have been unpopular with his apprentices while the barque was in Rio; he certainly treated them well.

When the *Garthpool* was being reloaded with her wheat, 1,500 bags were found to be damaged through the water that leaked into the barque. They were landed on the decks to be dumped overboard when she got right out to sea. The steering gear was repaired and she left on the 27th June.

Captain Wylie sailed the barque to a position in latitude 30° south, longitude 30° west, to avoid the south-setting current down the coast, and it was not until she was a week out that a course could be set to the northward for Falmouth. The south-east trade winds were picked up on the 11th July in latitude 16° 1′ south, longitude 26° 9′ west, and the equator was crossed a week later, the trade winds dying out on the 20th July in latitude 3° 9′ north, longitude 26° 9′ west.

When the correct chronometer time was ascertained on the 26th July, after getting their position from a German steamer, it was found that it had been giving the barque a position 60 miles in error in the longitude. The north-east trade winds were picked up on the 28th July, and that day was memorable for the *Garthpool* was tacked successfully, the only time on that passage.

Flores, in the Azores, was sighted on the 20th August and food began to run short. Treacle and tinned meat had already been finished and by the 21st August there was no sugar, butter, salt meat or coffee left. A week later the grain from the cargo was boiled for meals and was pronounced very good.

On the 4th September Bishop's Lighthouse, Scilly Islands, was abeam at 11 am, distance off 5 miles. A fishing boat came alongside and exchanged fresh fish for ship's biscuits. The next morning the *Garthpool* anchored in Falmouth Harbour and stores came aboard. By this time the crew were living on oatmeal and split peas. Orders came through to proceed to Liverpool and she sailed without a tug. After a pilot was picked up in Liverpool Bay, at 9 am on Saturday the 11th September, the barque was taken to anchor with 60 fathoms of cable out. A tug came out to the barque at one o'clock that afternoon and left immediately for Liverpool to get permission to tow the barque up river. She did not return, and as the weather deteriorated, a rough sea caused the barque to ship seas over the bulwarks on both sides. The barque lay at anchor all day on Sunday and at noon on Monday the 13th September, the anchor was hove-up by steam power from the donkey engine, and the *Garthpool* sailed up river, without the assistance of tugs, and anchored off New Brighton at 6.30 pm.

I do not know of a similar achievement in the United Kingdom, although I have served in a barque that sailed 40 miles up and down the Guayas River at Guayaquil in Ecuador. But the barque I served in was three-masted and much smaller and handier than the *Garthpool*. Captain

Wylie and the Liverpool pilot made history the day they sailed the *Garthpool* up the River Mersey without the help of tugs; and it is fitting that the last of the British windjammers should have that honour.

On the following day, the 14th September, 1926, the tug *Flying Breeze*, towed the *Garthpool* to Spillers and Bakers wharf at the Great Float, Birkenhead, for the discharge of her cargo. When the crew were paid off on the next day they were given an additional £2 as compensation for the shortage of food on the passage.

Young Williams, the apprentice, was promoted to third mate and shifted his gear from the half deck to the third mate's cabin aft. It was rather small, being only six feet long by five feet wide.

Captain Wylie left windjammers and went in command of one of the King Line steamers. Mr Macdonald, the first mate, retired from the sea, and later worked as a rigger on the Sydney Harbour Bridge when it was being built.

When young J D L Williams rejoined the *Garthpool* he found that Captain Thomson, late of the *Garthneill*, had been appointed to her command. The Captain had arrived in London only a fortnight before in the P & O Company's liner *Ballarat*, having returned from Adelaide. He was a teetotaller and a non-smoker but very fond of boiled sweets. Before the barque left, Mrs Thomson gave young Williams a sack of them done up in parcels with instructions that he was to put one by the Captain's plate at breakfast time on the first day of every month, on his birthday, and on certain other special days; but he was never to let the Captain know where they came from or he would find them and 'gobble' the lot. Captain Williams wrote to the author: 'This delightful lady left other parcels with other shipmates, and we all of us had our pleasant little surprises during the voyage.'

Captain Thomson was never idle and he hated idleness in others. His instructions to his mates on the employment of the crew was: 'Keep them on the go, mister, keep them on the go! If they sit on their arses they'll hatch out some mischief!' He abhorred waste. Every spoonful of galley slush was saved for grease, and every rope yarn saved for making bag-a-wrinkle, a mat used for preventing chafing of the sails against the wire stays. 'Sometimes,' wrote Captain Williams, 'this economy went too far; we saved lamp oil by not burning it in our side lights unless another ship was in sight.' This appears to have been not unusual in the last of the windjammers although it was not practised in the barques in which I served. There, one of the apprentices acted as lamptrimmer and the putting out and taking in of the sidelights was his responsibility and the officer of the watch saw that it was carried out at the correct times. Economy had to be practised in order to avoid, as much as possible, losses in the running of the last of the British windjammers; but the saving of oil at the risk of a collision was surely, as Captain Williams wrote, carrying it too far.

The first mate was William Loades, a West Countryman, sixty-eight years of age. He was marvellous for his age and from all accounts gave very satisfactory service. He held a master mariner's certificate and had been first mate under Captain Thomson in the *Garthneill*. Mr Loades first went to sea in the 1860s, was third mate at the age of 19 and carried straight on with his promotion to first mate. He yarned with young Williams, in the night watches, of his youth at sea and it was not much different from that experienced then in the *Garthpool*. Mr V W Martin, who came from Devon, now had his certificate and joined as second mate. He was a very able and aggressive officer with complete confidence in his ability of which he was well justified. It will be remembered that when third mate of the *Garthpool*, he had met with an accident on board at Dunkirk and could not sail in the barque. The half deck was full of apprentices, some making their first voyage to sea and others from John Stewart's barque *Kilmallie* which had arrived in London on the 14th September, 1926, on her last voyage before being broken up.

This voyage of the *Garthpool* started from Birkenhead on the 21st November, 1926, with an outward passage, in ballast, for Port Adelaide. Sir William Garthwaite now relied on a homeward cargo of wheat, which he had bought in Australia, to pay the running costs of the *Garthpool*. She towed out into the Irish Sea and the tug was cast off when Holyhead was abeam. Then she had to beat against a head wind and the crew of twenty-eight were sorely tested right from the start. Off the south coast of Ireland the barque encountered a strong southerly gale, and, in spite of all that could be done, she was set in towards the rock-bound coast near Cork. After an anxious night the wind shifted and allowed the barque to draw away from the danger.

Once the danger of a lee shore was past and the *Garthpool* was on her course to the southward, Captain Thomson shaved the hair off his head. From then on, till Adelaide was reached, he used neither razor, scissors nor hair brush, but let his hair and whiskers grow as they wished, which was at approximately the same speed, perpendicular to the surface and in several shades of grey. Three months later, at the end of the passage, his appearance was astounding but, such was the force of his personality, none of the crew dared to comment on it within his hearing.

After shaving his head the next thing he did was to go into the sail locker. He came out yelling for the third mate: 'Where are all the sails, mister?' he shouted. 'There's a lower topsail and a course, but, according to the inventory there should be a complete spare suit of sails!' The only answer that the third mate could give was that they had all blown out of their bolt ropes, in one storm or another, and had not been replaced. After this discovery Captain Thomson did his best to avoid bad weather and made sure of getting the sails fast on the yards in good time when gales could not be avoided. Even so it wasn't a bad passage for time out to Adelaide.

The equator was crossed twenty-seven days out from Birkenhead and down in the Roaring Forties of the South Indian Ocean the *Garthpool* logged 290 miles a day on occasions. She was sailing light in ballast, which helped considerably in those following gales and seas.

She arrived at Port Adelaide on the 8th March, 1927, after a passage of 102 days. A cargo of wheat was loaded there and the *Garthpool* sailed on the 6th April, 1927 for Queenstown for orders. Captain Thomson sailed to the westward across the Great Australian Bight, then to the northward into the south-east trade winds and round the Cape of Good Hope into the South Atlantic. He chose this route because of the finer weather which would put less strain on the barque. The author is sure that far more windjammers would have been sailed home that way if they had not met with westerly gales in the Great Australian Bight. Captain Thomson considered April a good month to cross the Bight to the westward and in the event he was right. He made the passage home in 128 days. Not a good one, but many made round Cape Horn averaged 120 days. In fact the previous passage made from Australia, via Cape Horn, had taken 196 days.

This passage home from Adelaide was made without sighting land. There was endless work to be done on board to keep the barque maintained satisfactorily, on deck and aloft. And, of course, there was the usual hauling of the yards round and setting and making sails fast. What surprised the author was that in the three years that Captain Williams served in the *Garthpool* he never saw a sail reefed. In the author's service in sail we reefed and shook the reef out a number of times when running the easting down. In one four-hour watch the main upper topsail was reefed twice.

The *Garthpool* met every kind of wind on the way home and on one occasion she was becalmed and remained motionless on a glassy sea for three days. There is nothing more annoying, disheartening or unnerving in a windjammer than this. Captain Thomson walked up and down the poop sometimes whistling shrilly out over the barque's stern, getting more and more badtempered until he would clench his fists, and, looking up at the sky, would shout: 'Don't sit up there grinning at me; give me a wind or come down on deck and have it out like a man!'

Captain Williams, writing to the author, remarked that he could never understand why they did not have a radio set on board. Many of the Scandinavian windjammers were fitted with receiving sets driven by small generators that were powered by a towed rotator. With this cheap set valuable weather reports and time signals could have been obtained, the latter being invaluable for correcting the chronometers and getting the right longitude for the ship's position.

When the *Garthpool* reached the Irish coast she was hove-to off Queenstown (Cork) Harbour and her orders were brought out to her. They were for Dublin. Mr Williams, the young third mate, as he was then, had finished his apprenticeship two days before the barque arrived and received three days' pay at the rate of £5 a month. He was unable to raise his fare to England and had to pawn his camera and watch to raise the money. He had £20 in a Post Office Savings Account from which he paid for his board and lodging and his school and examination fees. He then passed for second mate.

The last British Windjammer

The next voyage of the *Garthpool* was similar to the last, only this time she sailed from Dublin instead of Birkenhead. Captain Thomson and the first and second mates sailed in her again. She left Dublin on the 14th October, 1927, and arrived off Semaphore, Adelaide on the 12th January, 1928, after a passage of 91 days.

Lieutenant Commander B Penrose of Truro, Cornwall, made this round voyage and the author is grateful to him for his account of it. He had served as a cadet in the British India Company's vessels and later spent some time in coasting and short-sea trade sailing ships out of ports on the south-west coast of England. He also served in the wooden three-masted barque *Harmony* on her last voyage from London to the Labrador coast.

On this voyage of the *Garthpool* the fo'c'sle accommodated several well-educated young men who came from good families. Most of them went for the adventure of sailing on what might well be, and, in fact was, the last British commercial windjammer, Cape Horner, to sail round the world; although this was not her last voyage. Bernard Penrose was the son of the Hon Mrs Penrose. The late James Martin, who signed on as an ordinary seaman, had resigned his commission in the Grenadier Guards to sail in the *Garthpool*. One of Martin's watchmates wrote this of him:

> He was a big man but very quiet and gentle with deep, profound thoughts and emotions which he did his best to conceal. He was obviously different, and in many ways superior, to the ordinary man and was admired and respected by all hands.

Early in the Second World War he was the first lieutenant of a 'Q' ship in command of Captain A E D Rider, VC, which was lost with all hands, except Captain Rider, when she went into action with a German submarine.

Two other members of the fo'c'sle crew on that voyage were professional seamen carving out their career in the Merchant Navy. Captain Frank Walker, who had previously made the outward passage in the *Garthneill*, was now an able seaman, and Captain J A McBrearty, of

Bromborough, Cheshire, also served in the *Garthpool* on that voyage. The four mentioned were all in the starboard watch. On this outward passage William G E Garthwaite, aged 21, the son of the owner, served as a cadet. He left the barque at Port Adelaide, signing off on the 19th January, 1928.

The usual trade winds and doldrums weather were experienced, and, when the *Garthpool* reached the position of the strong westerly winds and gales of the 'Roaring Forties', she showed that she was still capable of good speed when running before the wind in ballast. Lt Cdr Penrose claims that she logged 16 knots in two successive watches. The author knows that many windjammer men will disagree with this claim, but it is certain that she averaged twelve knots for two consecutive days. It was during this time that a tragedy occurred that marred the passage.

Early one morning, when the starboard watch were snug in their bunks, they were awakened by that dreaded shout 'Man Overboard!' They were out 'in a shot' hauling on a few clothes when the order came 'All hands on deck!' A young ordinary seaman had fallen into the sea off the footrope on the lee-side of the main yard.

Penrose, Martin, Walker and McBrearty, went aft and got into the lee lifeboat which was swung out in the davits and lowered down the barque's side. They did their best to fend her off from the side plating. Penrose broke one of his ankles in the attempt, but the barque was rolling so heavily that it was an impossibility to keep her clear. The gunwale was stove in, and, when she was lowered to sea level, it was found that she was leaking badly. The best report of an accident of this severity is always written in the vessel's Official Log Book by the master and here it is:

> 14th December, 1927. 6.15 am latitude 45° 22′ south, longitude 28° 42′ east. Whilst J Maddock, OS (ordinary seaman) was loosing the port [lee] side of the mainsail he slipped, missed his hold, and fell into the sea. A lifebuoy was immediately thrown to him from the poop, but he didn't get it. The ship [barque] at this time was going 12 knots by patent log. A strong breeze was blowing, the weather being misty. The barometer was down to 29.18 inches, the breeze was increasing and there was a considerable sea running. The fore

> and main topgallant sails were set, also the mizzen lower topgallant sail. In spite of the strong breeze and threatening conditions of the weather the helm was put down immediately and the ship [barque] brought [head] to the wind. Main and mizzen sails were [thrown] aback. All hands were called on deck and the port [lee side] lifeboat was swung out and lowered to the rail and eventually to the water. By this time the ship [barque] had sailed and drifted [with the wind and sea] a considerable distance.
>
> Although the second officer [mate] and the master were looking through glasses [binoculars] nothing could be seen of the man. As the wind was increasing and the sea rising, I didn't think it prudent to send the boat away as it would only be risking more lives. So the boat was hoisted on board and the ship [barque] put on her course.

The four seamen who got into the lifeboat to go to the rescue of their shipmate were volunteers and there was never any lack of these in a windjammer where a shipmate's life was involved, however great the risk. As has been stated already the master must make the decision as to whether the volunteers shall be allowed to go to the rescue.

It may be considered that Captain Thomson was too venturesome in ordering the mainsail to be loosed for setting at a time when the weather was worsening and a considerable sea was running, as well as the low reading of the barometer. It is difficult to criticise a master with such long experience, bearing in mind that he had made one complete voyage in the *Garthpool* and knew her capabilities.

On the following day, the burial service was read by the Captain in memory of the young ordinary seaman who was lost. An Inquiry was held at Port Adelaide on the 16th January, 1928 by the Superintendent of the Mercantile Marine Office. He reported.:

> I am of the opinion that the seaman fell from the main yard (in the execution of his duty) into the sea and was drowned. The evidence indicates that the weather was such that the lifeboat, although lowered, could not be sailed or pulled direct to windward to where the seaman fell overboard. Nor could the ship (in ballast) beat to

windward under the existing weather conditions and effect a rescue. There is no reason to believe any of the ship's gear is defective. Everything that could be done to effect a rescue under the circumstances appears to have been done by the master, officers and crew of the vessel in question.

It was not until young Penrose's ankle had been thoroughly examined that it was found to be fractured and was put into splints. However it had to be reset by a doctor in Adelaide. This was compensated by the fact that he was the only crew member to get shore leave while the barque lay at anchor in Semaphore. She left on the 6th February, 1928, to sail round into Spencer Gulf to load wheat in bags at Wallaroo, arriving on the 13th February. While the *Garthpool* was lying alongside the wharf there, at 10.30 am on the 20th February, apprentice Arthur Reeves fell 26 feet down No 1 hold when putting the hatches on. Fortunately the ballast in the bottom of the hold broke his fall. His head was cut in two places and his back was strained. First aid was given and a doctor came on board to attend to him. He was sent to the local hospital and returned to the barque on the 17th March and resumed his duties.

The *Garthpool* left Wallaroo for Queenstown on the 23rd March, 1928. Captain Thomson intended to make the passage home across the Great Australian Bight and round the Cape of Good Hope as he had done on the previous voyage. In fact the ss *Nestor* was signalled on the 2nd April, when ten days out, in latitude 35° 23′ south, longitude 122° 2′ east. After spending over a fortnight trying to reach and round Cape Leeuwin, Captain Thomson gave it up, squared the yards, and ran the barque to the eastward towards Cape Horn. This was not looked forward to by the occupants of the fo'c'sle and they improvised bogey stoves from paint drums and burnt the coal left over in the donkey boiler bunker.

Sails were split and torn into shreds during the passage to the 'Horn' and Captain Thomson organised his school of sailmaking and repaired them, making new sails where necessary. A new mainsail made in the limited confines of the after saloon was an achievement. The seas were mountainous and oil was used frequently to break their surface. Usually a full canvas oil bag, pricked with sail needles, was towed from either side of the fo'c'sle head in the bows. Another method was to stuff oakum down the lavatories, under the fo'c'sle head, and pour oil down on top of it. This gave good results. The worst gale came with winds of almost hurricane force in which only a goose-winged (half-set) fore lower topsail could be carried. Three of the bottle screws of the starboard fore shrouds pulled away from their anchor plate but the shrouds were secured with chains and did not carry away.

'All hands on deck!' was the order many times and there was little sleep for the watch below. On more than one occasion the galley was washed out and no hot food could be prepared for days. Sickness occurred in the half-deck and fo'c'sles and one seaman lost the fingers of his right hand when surging a jumping wire round the barrel of a capstan.

Captain Thomson gave young Penrose a bottle of brandy to help keep out the cold. He shared this with two of his watchmates. It was so helpful that the Captain passed five or six bottles altogether to young Penrose down in those freezing latitudes. This was most unusual. 'Splice the main brace!' was an order for all hands to go aft for a tot of rum, which was whacked out by the steward, but to give an individual a whole bottle was asking for drunkenness at a time when sobriety was essential. The reason was, of course, that the fo'c'sle housed an entirely different type of seamen who could be trusted to take the warming fluid in moderation, and Captain Thomson knew this. In any case the bottles were given out at the end of slop chest time after every other member of the crew had left the saloon. It seems unlikely that they were a gift, but whether a gift or paid for, I have never heard of any other case of a sailing ship master giving out spirits to a member of the crew a bottle at a time. Those young men in the fo'c'sle certainly impressed Captain Thomson and it is certain they were first-rate seamen.

In the fine weather of the South Atlantic all sail was crowded on in the south-east trade winds and Lt Cdr Penrose informed the author that an old topsail was secured to the foot of the foresail to give more sail area, and even the lifeboat and gig sails were hoisted in an effort to get more speed out of the barque. Shades of the stunsails of the old tea clippers!

Something else happened on that passage home which the author has never heard of before; cockroach racing. There were cockroaches in the half deck and fo'c'sle of the *Garthpool*, as there were in most windjammers. The finest specimens were chosen, painted with racing colours, and put in tracks in long, glass-covered boxes. A piece of food, liked by cockroaches, was placed at the far end of the track and they were released simultaneously to start their race. This diversion took place in the tropics north of the equator.

Stores ran short in the North Atlantic and the apprentices used a coffee grinder to grind the wheat into a powder from which the cook made porridge and flap jacks which were fried in rancid salt meat fat; yet they tasted good to those hungry sailors. Bread of a kind was also made from the ground wheat.

The Azores were the first land to be sighted since the *Garthpool* left Australia. This was on the 4th August. The next land seen was the lovely green coastline of Ireland which was approached one beautiful, warm, sunny day in August when all sail was set except the mizzen upper topgallant sail; the yard was rotten and the sail could not be set.

The *Garthpool* anchored off Queenstown on the 14th August, 1928, after a passage of 144 days. Orders were received for Belfast and the barque left in tow on the 20th August. There being a fair wind, all sail was set to help and the *Garthpool* arrived on the 22nd August, 1928. Sailing with Lt Cdr Penrose on this voyage was Lt Cdr H V Howard. They are both 'Cape Horners', and met once again, nearly forty years later, at the Annual Dinner of the British Section of the Cape Horners in the Connaught Rooms in London. I wonder what they talked about!

The *Garthpool* sailed, once again in ballast, for Australia to bring home another cargo of wheat. She left Belfast on the 5th October, 1928, for Port Adelaide. Captain Thomson was her master and Mr Loades her first mate. She had a new second mate, Mr F S J Butcher of Hull. He had served his apprenticeship in Sir William Garthwaite's barques and full-rigged ships and was on board the *Garthforce* when she hit the iceberg. Mr Alfred J Pazolt, marine artist of Boston, Mass, USA, then aged 57, sailed in her as purser at a wage of a shilling a month and gave a detailed account of the outward passage.

The *Garthpool* went round the north of Ireland into the North Atlantic. At 10 am on the 7th October, when the barque was in latitude 56° 52′ north, longitude 50° 48′ west, the first mate found five stowaways in the sail locker. Captain Thomson resolved not to carry them to Australia and would have diverted the barque to Queenstown to land them if necessary. Fortunately a Fleetwood trawler was sighted and signalled and she altered course to the *Garthpool*. The stowaways were transferred to her in one of the barque's lifeboats. That night very bad weather was experienced and sail had to be reduced to three lower topsails. Then at ten o'clock on the following morning four more stowaways were found. There is no word of their being transferred to another vessel or being put ashore.

Head winds and heavy gales were encountered in the North Atlantic. There were only three of the crew in the fo'c'sle who had been to sea in a sailing ship before and the fact that they dealt with the considerable amount of taking in and making sail fast, besides the trimming of the yards and wearing ship in the head winds so early on the passage, is very much to their credit. On one occasion when the fore upper topgallant sail was being hoisted by capstan the sea shanty 'O'Roving' was attempted by one of the crew, but it was such a failure that Captain Thomson went along to the fore deck, took his place on a capstan bar, and, pushing round with the men, showed them how it should be sung. They joined in delightedly.

On the 12th October, in latitude 53° 6′ north, longitude 15° 48′ west, apprentice Richard Allman was laid up with pains in his back and seemed to be getting worse. He was losing the use of his limbs and had a slight fever. His limbs were rubbed with liniment.

On the 14th October Captain Thomson reported that he was worse and had no control over his limbs or bladder. He was given liquid nourishment and his limbs were rubbed with spirit and liniment. His condition was the same two days later and he had a high temperature. On the 18th October he was getting worse and became paralysed and had no power in any part of his body. He was given liquid refreshment when he could take it.

He passed away at thirty-five minutes past noon on the 19th October, 1928, in latitude 45° north, longitude 9° 36′ west.

On the 20th October, 1928, the last entry in the Official Log Book concerning apprentice Richard Allman was made:

> 9 am in latitude 44° 50′ north, longitude 9° 47′ west. Buried this day at 9 am with all due ceremony.'

Mr Pazolt's recording of the burial cannot be omitted:

> This morning at 8 am the gale is still howling and there is a huge sea running. At 9 am the apprentice was buried. All hands were called aft and the Captain read the burial service. It was a most impressive scene on the rolling, windswept poop with the Captain standing beside the flag-covered body and the silent crew, all grouped around, swaying against the steep angle of the deck and masts. Just then a ray of sunshine came through a break in the ragged, leaden, storm clouds, spreading a silver light over the huge tumbling seas.

An Inquiry was held at Port Adelaide into the sad loss by the Superintendent of the Mercantile Marine Offices and he agreed that Captain Thomson did everything possible to save the lad's life. Even so the Captain was badly depressed for some time after his death.

On the eighth day out when the barque was in latitude 53° 24′ north, longitude 16° 23′ west, the wind freshened from the south-west and the topgallant sails were made fast on the yards. Immediately after, the upper topsails were made fast and when the mainsail, the largest sail on board, was taken in, all hands except the man at the wheel went aloft to help make it fast on the yard. This included both the mates, and even the captain went aloft to help. The captain was then sixty-two years of age and the first mate was sixty-four. That's a great age to be working aloft on a wire footrope in a howling gale of wind. It was getting increasingly difficult to get hands with enough experience to handle sails aloft and the 'greenhorns' in the crew were then only eight days out. Give them another month and they would not want their captain's help aloft. The *Garthpool* was now the only British windjammer afloat, for John Stewart's *William Mitchell* had been sold to shipbreakers in September, 1928.

On the 23rd October, sixteen days out from Belfast, the *Garthpool* had been driven back to the latitude of Ushant. A gale was blowing as it had been nearly all the time since they had left Belfast. The fact that the barque was in ballast with her bulwarks high out of the water prevented the crew from enduring the dangers and discomfort of heavy seas breaking on board, but water did come over on to the fore and main decks consequent on the heavy rolling of the barque. On this day the mizzen upper topsail, the main staysail and the big foresail (a new sail) blew out of their bolt ropes to ribbons.

On Saturday the 27th October, the wind was in excess of force 9; but, at last, on the next day, there was a change in the weather, and with all sail set the *Garthpool* made a good day's run to the southward of 247 miles. The Captain had his 'sewing bee' and everyone who could use a palm and needle was on the poop stitching away 'hell for leather', repairing the sails.

On the morning of the 31st October, Madeira Island was passed so close that the cliffs and beautiful green valleys with red-roofed houses could be seen from the barque. Two days later she passed the Canary Islands and picked up the north-east trade winds which later served her well with a ten-knot breeze.

In latitude 7° 44′ north, longitude 22° west, on the 8th November, the trade winds died out and the *Garthpool* entered the doldrums with its light variable winds, calms, and torrential rains. The scupper holes were blocked to hold the rain water on deck, between the bulwarks, and the crew bathed and washed their clothes. Then clean rain water was collected in buckets, as it ran off the poop deck, and poured into tanks and barrels for future use.

A noteworthy event of this passage was when the white painted German sail training ship *Grosshezogen Elizabeth* on her way to Bahia, Brazil, passed the *Garthpool* in latitude 3° north, longitude 25° 11′ west. By this time the barque had picked up the south-east trade winds.

Although the equator was crossed on Thursday the 13th November, the celebrations were not carried out until the afternoon of the following Saturday, when no work was done about the decks. 'Father Neptune' came on board and twelve members of the crew, who were crossing the equator for the first time, were lathered and shaved with the carpenter's huge, wooden razor, dosed with soap pills and ducked in a big bath on deck which had been constructed with canvas and wooden supports. Then the victims were presented with their certificates by 'Father Neptune'.

Sports were held on the main deck that afternoon which included obstacle, sack, potato, pick-a-back and wheelbarrow races, rope climbing and a boxing display. At six o'clock that evening a concert was held under the boat skids on the after main deck. It was something to be remembered. Mandolin solos were played and this instrument was, on occasions, also used for accompanying songs. Ballads, always liked by seafarers, and sea songs, were accompanied by a concertina and a mouth organ. South Sea Island melodies, accompanied by a Hawaiian guitar, were probably the most popular of all. And the carpenter performed on one of his big saws. It was unusual to have all this musical talent on a windjammer, and one person on board suggested that the crew were better musicians than sailors. It was an unrehearsed concert such as could only be heard on a ship's deck in the tropics where the music was enhanced by the beauty of the night. It finished with 'Auld Lang Syne' and three cheers for the captain and the mates. Did Captain Thomson give the order to 'splice the main brace?' It is certain that he did!

The south-east trade winds were lost on Sunday, the 25th November, in latitude 33° 30′ south, longitude 26° west. This was further south than usual and reduced the time of waiting for the strong westerlies that would drive the barque through the Roaring Forties to Australia. The birds of the southern seas appeared now, including the lordly albatross with a span of fourteen feet from tip to tip of wing, the smaller mollyhawks and the Cape pigeons.

A large iceberg was sighted on the starboard bow, 8 miles distant, in latitude 43° 12′ south, longitude 11° 14′ west at 1.30 pm on the 7th

December. It was estimated to be 180 feet high and 650 feet in length. The weather had turned very cold and visibility was poor.

When another iceberg was sighted on the next morning, Captain Thomson decided to make to the northward to get away from the northern fringe of the icebergs. Even so the ship was in latitude 42° south when at seven in the morning on the 11th December, another large iceberg was passed close to, and on the next day when the barque was further north still, in 41° 30′ south, another was passed only half a mile away. It was described as 'gleaming white with vivid blue cracks, fissures and caverns'. Captain Thomson said that he had never known so many icebergs so far north.

On the 13th December, by the patent log, the *Garthpool* was making a speed of fifteen knots, which the author thinks was probably her best. The famous 'P' line four-masted barques, owned by Laiez of Hamburg, achieved speeds of 18 knots. Their captains reported that to set more sail, when that speed was reached, only buried their barque's bows in the sea, and reduced their speed. It seems probable that without the help of current or tide, 18 knots was the maximum for a big four-masted barque.

On Sunday the 16th December, in latitude 43° 52′ south, longitude 41° 22′ east Mr Pazolt reported the barque's record day's run as 319 nautical miles. The time for that run, as the vessel was sailing to the eastward, would be about 23 hours 30 minutes which gives an average speed of about 13½ knots. On this passage the *Garthpool* had more than her fair share of very bad weather. The days when strong gales caused sail to be shortened down to lower topsails were far too frequent. When, on several occasions, I ran the easting down it was possible to keep the upper topsails and foresail set day after day to give our barque that 'grand push' which the windjammer captains loved. I maintain that the best crossings were made in about latitude 40° south.

At noon on Christmas Day the *Garthpool* was in latitude 44° 24′ south, longitude 93° 43′ east. It was celebrated in a much more joyous way than in my time in windjammers. Christmas presents were given to all members of the crew by one of the mates who was preceded along the deck at midnight on Christmas Eve by one of the apprentices who carried a hurricane lamp. Carols were sung and very special meals were issued to all hands.

The barque sailed close to Cape Borda lighthouse to receive orders. It was for Port Adelaide as was expected and she arrived on the 5th January, 1929. The passage took 92 days which was quite a good one considering the delay experienced at the start. The *Garthpool* loaded a full cargo of wheat in bags for Hull and sailed on the 6th March, 1929. She called at Queenstown on the 18th July after a long passage of 134 days and there her orders were confirmed and she sailed to Hull arriving on the 2nd August, 1929.

Her next voyage was from Hull to Australia in ballast to load wheat. The same captain and two mates sailed in her and M L Newmary of London, aged 28, was her third mate. He held a second mate's certificate. The *Garthpool* had been completely overhauled in Hull and was fitted with a new jib boom and new fore lower topsail and mizzen upper topgallant yards. The crew were all British with the exception of a French sailor named Jean Glovo. The bosun, Mr Cherionoweth, had sailed to the Antarctic in Scott's *Discovery* and had served for several years in Dundee whalers and later as bosun in the famous British full-rigged ship *Mount Stewart*. The cook came from Mauritius and had served for many years in the 'Inver' Line barques of George Milne of Aberdeen. The carpenter came from Aberdeen and the sailmaker from Australia. Again the crew in the fo'c'sle were superior to the average fo'c'sle crowd. There were two River Humber apprentice pilots getting their square-rigged time in for their pilotage certificates, George Hocart, an ex sub-lieutenant, from the submarine service, two young seamen with second mate's certificates, and a young ordinary seaman who had served in Lord Brassey's yacht, *Sunbeam*. There was also a French-Canadian who had made a voyage in the *Archibald Russell* and two young men from Cork in Ireland making their first voyage to sea; they were Charles Dowman, a bank clerk, and Tod O'Sullivan.

No 8 on the Crew List in the barque's Articles of Agreement was Stan Hugill, able seaman of Hoylake, then aged 22. He was the shantyman on board and was, in fact, the last shantyman on board a British windjammer. This is a notable achievement in itself, but he has done better; he has written excellent books. *Shanties from the Seven Seas* is undoubtedly the best book written on sea-shanties, and *Sailortown*, which describes the old haunts of the windjammer sailor ashore in the world's ports, including the pubs and the 'red light' districts, is unequalled. Both books are illustrated with Stan's full page nautical line drawings; the best of their kind I have seen.

Mr A J Pazolt, who made the outward passage to Port Adelaide on the last voyage, joined the barque again. With him were the well-known yachtsman, Major Peter Kerr Smiley, and Mr W M Hutton. They signed on as pursers at a shilling a month. The apprentices on this voyage were: W N Basson, aged 17, of Hemel Hempstead, Hertfordshire, E E Fenwick, aged 15, of Hull, W A Wills, aged 15, of Belfast, T R Mines, aged 17, of Cambridge, E J Smith, aged 17, of Port Adelaide, R G B Harrison, aged 17, of Newport, Mon, T H B Oates, aged 19, of Johannesburg, South Africa, and J W Kinney, aged 19, of Hawaii. Of these lads the last named is at the time of writing Captain J W Kinney, Marine Superintendent of the Delta Steamship Lines Inc of New Orleans, USA. He obtained his British Master's certificate with square-rigged endorsement and his United States of America Master's Licence, Unlimited. All the apprentices were making their first voyage to sea except Kinney who had made the previous voyage in the *Garthpool*. The crew, including the mates, the apprentices and the Captain, numbered thirty-four. This was a big crew for a windjammer at that time; even for a big four-masted barque.

In the Articles of Agreement for this voyage, dated the 17th October, 1929, the name of the Company was given as The Marine Navigation Company of Canada Limited, of 1–2, Board of Trade Buildings, 42nd Street, Montreal, Canada. Her port of registry was Montreal and she wore the red ensign of the Canadian Merchant Navy.

The *Garthpool* left Alexander Dock, Hull, in tow of the tug *Seaman* on the 23rd October, 1939, bound for Cape Borda, Kangaroo Island, South Australia, in ballast, for orders. After leaving, a gale warning was received by wireless on the tug and the barque was anchored for the night in the shelter of Yarmouth Roads. On the next day the tow was renewed and the *Garthpool* was towed as far as Beachy Head when sail was set and the tug returned to Hull.

After the topsails had been set Stan Hugill and a young seaman named Fuller went aloft to loose the main topgallant sails preparatory to setting them. After loosing the upper topgallant sail Hugill saw that the tugmaster was waiting to take letters from the barque for posting when he got back to Hull; so he slid down the backstay to the deck to get his and Fuller's letters to hand over to the tug. As he came up out of the fo'c'sle, which was just abaft the mainmast, with them, there was a crash and chains, blocks and ropes came hurtling down from aloft narrowly missing the crew standing near the mainmast on the midship-section deck.

When Hugill looked aloft he was relieved to see that young Fuller was standing in the topgallant rigging, clear of the mast. The yard had been hoisted with the donkey engine, the chain attached to the yard had carried away and the yard had crashed down on to the wire lifts which, happily, had held it from falling down on to the deck. While still in the English Channel the approach of a gale gave the hands their first experience of making sail fast in bad weather, and later on, when the wind went round and blew from ahead, they wore ship for the first time.

On Sunday the 27th October a fair wind took the barque down the Channel with all sail set. This time the upper topgallant yards were hoisted by hand capstan, the capstan bars being shipped and the crew tramping round to the tunes of sea shanties. Hugill reported that the food was good and there was a frequent issue of bread baked on board. Once clear of the Channel the *Garthpool* encountered several days of head winds and when a fair wind did come the crew squared the yards and the barque made to the southward.

By day the crew overhauled the barque's gear, giving due attention to the footropes under the yards. These are wire ropes which could, by breaking under the weight of the seamen standing on them, send them crashing to the deck below or into the sea. Then there was the never-ending job of chipping and scraping the rusted steelwork of the houses and bulwarks prior to red-leading and painting them. That was only one of the many jobs carried out by the watches between bracing the yards and handing the sails. In the second dog-watch (6 pm to 8 pm), when the watches were able to get together in one of the fo'c'sles, they enjoyed a musical evening. They had a gramophone and records, which I never saw in the windjammers in which I served; but they preferred to provide their own music. The submarine lieutenant played the violin, the Frenchman the accordion and one of the apprentice pilots played the banjo ukulele. They all sang; or, at least, had a go.

On Thursday the 7th November, Puerto Santo was sighted, and, later that day, Madeira. The north-east trade wind was sending the *Garthpool* along at a good twelve knots. On the next day she sailed between the islands of Palma and Teneriffe in the Canary Islands. The wind had increased and was now driving the barque along at thirteen knots.

On the morning of the 11th November, Armistice Day, at eleven o'clock, Greenwich Mean Time, 9.30 am ship's time, the ensign was dipped to half mast, and, with all hands mustered aft on the poop, the two minutes' silence was observed in latitude 17° 40′ north, longitude 22° 25′ west. At 4.30 pm that afternoon Sal Island, one of the Cape Verde Islands, was abeam. The distance off could not be obtained with any accuracy as the weather was hazy.

At 9.25 that night a sudden shout of 'All hands on deck!' brought the starboard watch tumbling out from below. The port watch were hauling the yards round, and, fine on the bow to leeward, high land could be seen through the hazy mist. Almost immediately the look-out on the fo'c'sle head shouted: 'Breakers ahead!'

Up went the wheel and the sharp slatting of canvas was heard as the yards came rattling round. The barque was wore round in the hope of clearing the rocks. As the mizzen yards were being hauled round it felt as if the barque was sliding over a reef. When the crew went along to the main braces the look-out shouted 'Surf ahead!' The main brace had just been taken off the belaying pin when the barque crashed on to the reef with a lurch to port. Everything on board shook. The main brace was made fast quickly and the hands rushed for the shelter of the donkey house for it seemed that the masts and yards must crash down about their heads on to the deck.

The barque lurched over more to port and bumped heavily on the reef. It was impossible to back her off, for the big sea that was running, consequent on the strong trade winds and the heavy ground swell, held her fast. Looking down the holds it was seen that the water was up to the 'tween decks. There was no hope for the barque. Captain Thomson gave the order: 'All hands abandon ship!' This was a difficult and hazardous operation in the starboard lifeboat, for the barque was lying over with a heavy list to port. The boat had to be helped down the sloping side of the barque into the water.

After the two boats had cleared the barque and the reef, the numbers in them were equalled and the boats' sails were hoisted. They made for Boavista Island in the darkness of the night but could not find a landing place. They had tried to make the small port of Sal Rei, got into a dangerous surf-ridden bay, and had had to get out of it to clear water to anchor. At dawn two natives swam out and directed them to a small bay at Cantao in Boavista Island where they had to anchor again. Two shallow native craft took the shipwrecked crew from the boats to the shore where they landed at the 'Look Out Post'. This was a 'tumble-down' shanty, the lower rooms being swept out to accommodate the crew. The natives were mulattos, something like West African negroes, who spoke Portuguese. They had ridden on donkeys from the nearby fishing village which consisted of six adobe houses with turfed roofs.

Captain Thomson, Mr Butcher, the second mate, George Hocart and four other members of the crew went back to the wreck in one of the lifeboats but the heavy swell prevented them from boarding her. The boat was driven to leeward and had to be beached. There appeared to be no drinking water at Cantao but a Spanish steamer, the *Axbe-Mendi*, that had been wrecked on another reef, had been loaded with about 100,000 bottles of champagne cider, which the natives had salvaged and now gave the shipwrecked mariners to drink.

On the next day Captain Thomson and Mr Butcher, with a Portuguese Customs officer, rode across the island on donkeys to the small port of Sal Rei, which was about 17½ miles across the mountains. That day some members of the crew boarded the *Garthpool* to find her just a mess of wreckage. She had been looted and all their gear had been taken.

At Cantao their food consisted of ship's biscuits and condensed milk, which they had brought in the lifeboats, and the champagne cider. They stayed there for two days and then were sailed round to Sal Rei in a cutter of about 80 tons. The Mauritius cook from the *Garthpool* went into the cutter's galley and produced an excellent meal of ham and eggs and tea for all hands, and one of the purser-passengers opened a packed case of luxuries from Fortnum and Mason, which he had been saving, and gave each member of the crew some cold soup, a slice of bottled chicken and other attractive eatables.

On the 16th November the same cutter took them all to the island of St Vincent, about 130 miles away, where they were landed at midday on Sunday the 17th November. The seamen were accommodated at John Oliveiras' London Bar. He had been a sailor in English ships and could speak English fluently. There they had a wonderful meal of bacon and eggs, the British sailor's ideal, and were able to wash, shave and put on clean clothes. Stan Hugill wrote with enthusiasm of their treatment there: 'The native house-girls washed all our clothes and looked after us as though we were a crowd of tourists instead of shipwrecked mariners.'

The Western Telegraph Company's staff invited them to their quarters and they, and the British Consul, joined in the sea-shanty singing by the crew. Incidentally, for anyone interested, 'Fire down below' was the last sea-shanty sung on the *Garthpool*, the last of the British windjammers.

Wilson's Coal Company also gave great hospitality to the crew who spent pleasant evenings with them. Captain Thomson, the second mate, the three pursers and the apprentices went home on the passenger liner, *Avelona Star*, and the rest of the crew followed on the next day on the Royal Mail Steam Packet's *Deseado*.

Although there was an attempt by Sir William Garthwaite and some prominent Merchant Navy captains, including Sir Selwyn Day, to form a 'Sea Lion Sail Training Society', it did not materialise. At the early committee meetings it was revealed that an annual loss had been made on the ships and barques of Sir William's Marine Navigation Company, and it would be necessary to rely on a Government grant or voluntary contributions. The outline of the scheme was to obtain a sum of money by public subscription to build a square-rigged, ocean-going, sailing ship for the training of cadets. The approximate cost was estimated to be £50,000. An alternative suggestion was to purchase a second-hand windjammer for about £10,000. It was proposed that the vessel should make annual round voyages from Britain to Australia with cargoes.

It was not to be and the *Garthpool* remains the last British windjammer to sail the seven seas.

Fleet of Marine Navigation Co

Vessel	*Rig Material*	*Date built*	*Date bought*	*Net tons*	*Dimensions in feet Length*	*Breadth*	*Depth*	*Hulked, broken up or sunk*
Queen Elizabeth	Ship Steel	1889	1915	1707	252.7	40.1	22.5	Sunk Dec 1915
Carnmoney	3 mst. barque Iron	1884	1915	1255	235.5	32.6	21	Sunk May 1917
Invercauld	3 mst. barque Steel	1891	1916	1303	237.5	36.2	21.7	Sunk Feb 1917
Invermay	3 mst. barque Steel	1895	1916	1337	238	36	21.7	Sunk April 1917
Garthneill	3 mst. barque Steel	1895	1916	1340	238	36	21.7	Hulked Aug 1926
Garthsnaid	3 mst. barque Steel	1892	1916	1312	238	36.2	21.7	Hulked June 1923
Garthpool	4 mst. barque Steel	1891	1917	2652	310	45	25	Wrecked Nov 1929
Garthforce	Ship Steel	1892	1917	1859	267.9	39.7	23.4	Broken up Nov 1926
Garthwray	Ship Steel	1889	1917	1791	264	39	23.6	Wrecked April 1924
Garthgarry	3 mst. barque Steel	1891	1918	1309	237.5	36.2	21.5	Broken up June 1924

Maps of the West Coast of South America and Cape Horn and Rigs of the vessels of the Garth Line.

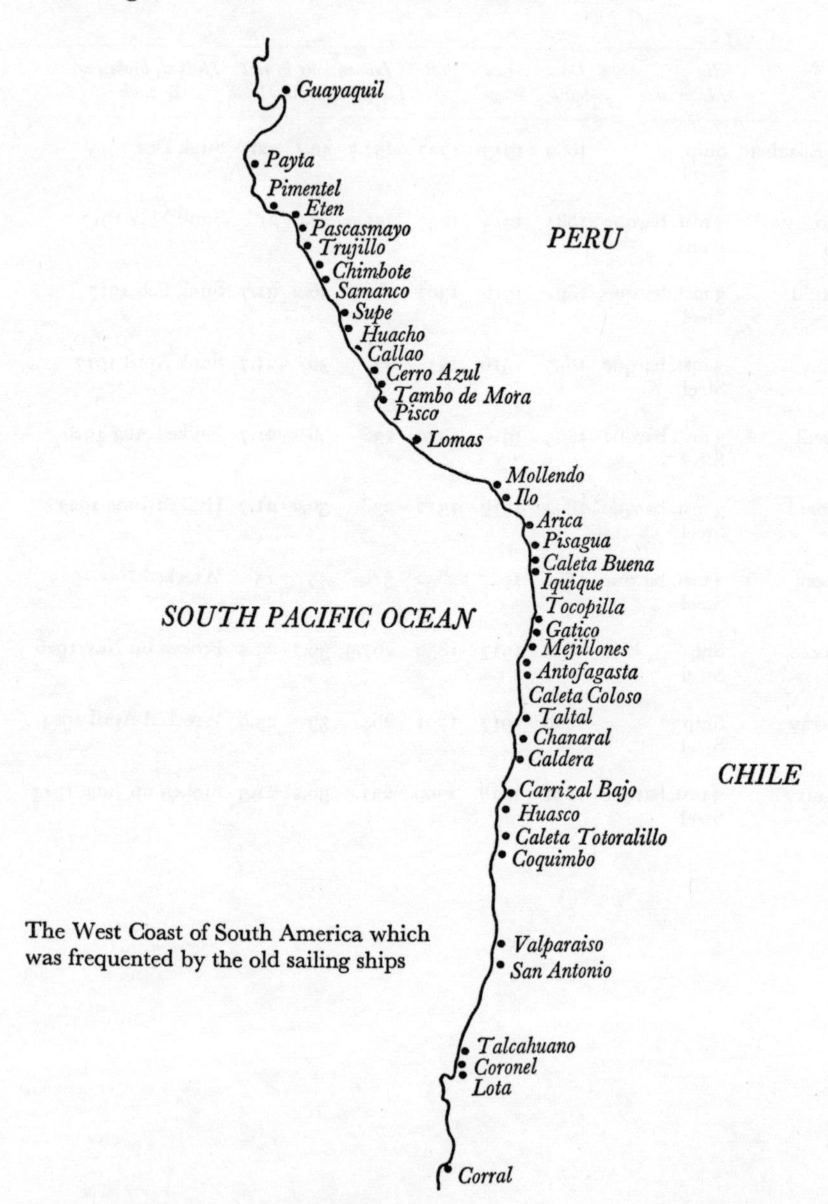

The West Coast of South America which was frequented by the old sailing ships

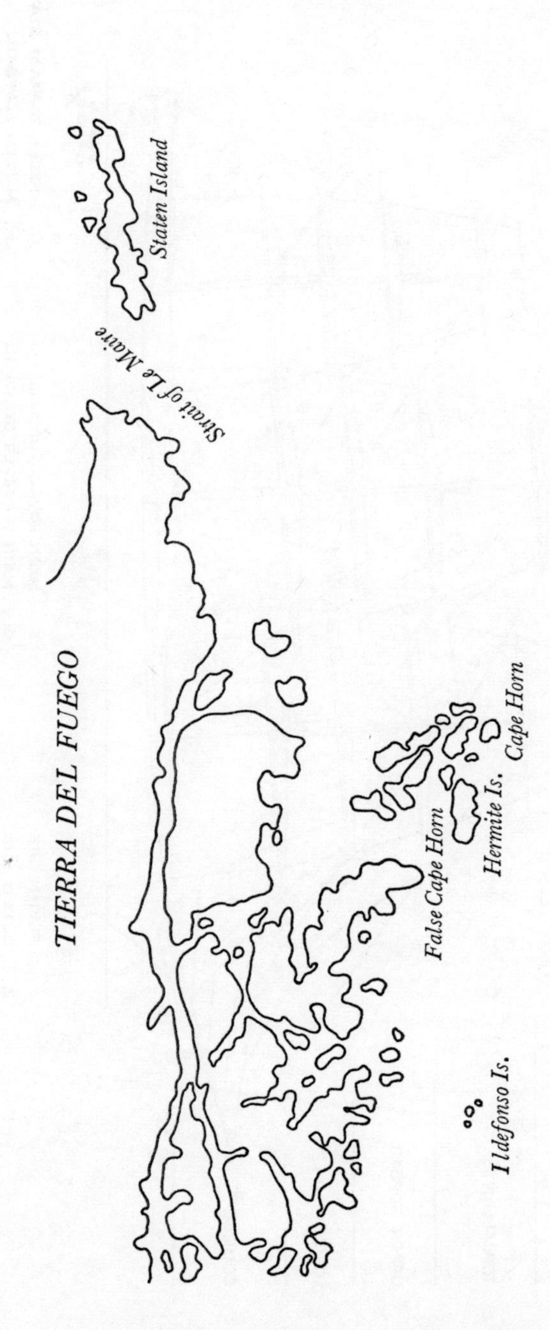

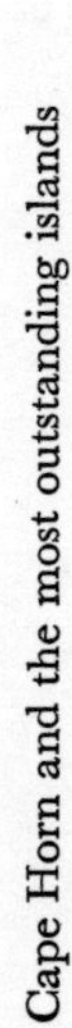
Cape Horn and the most outstanding islands

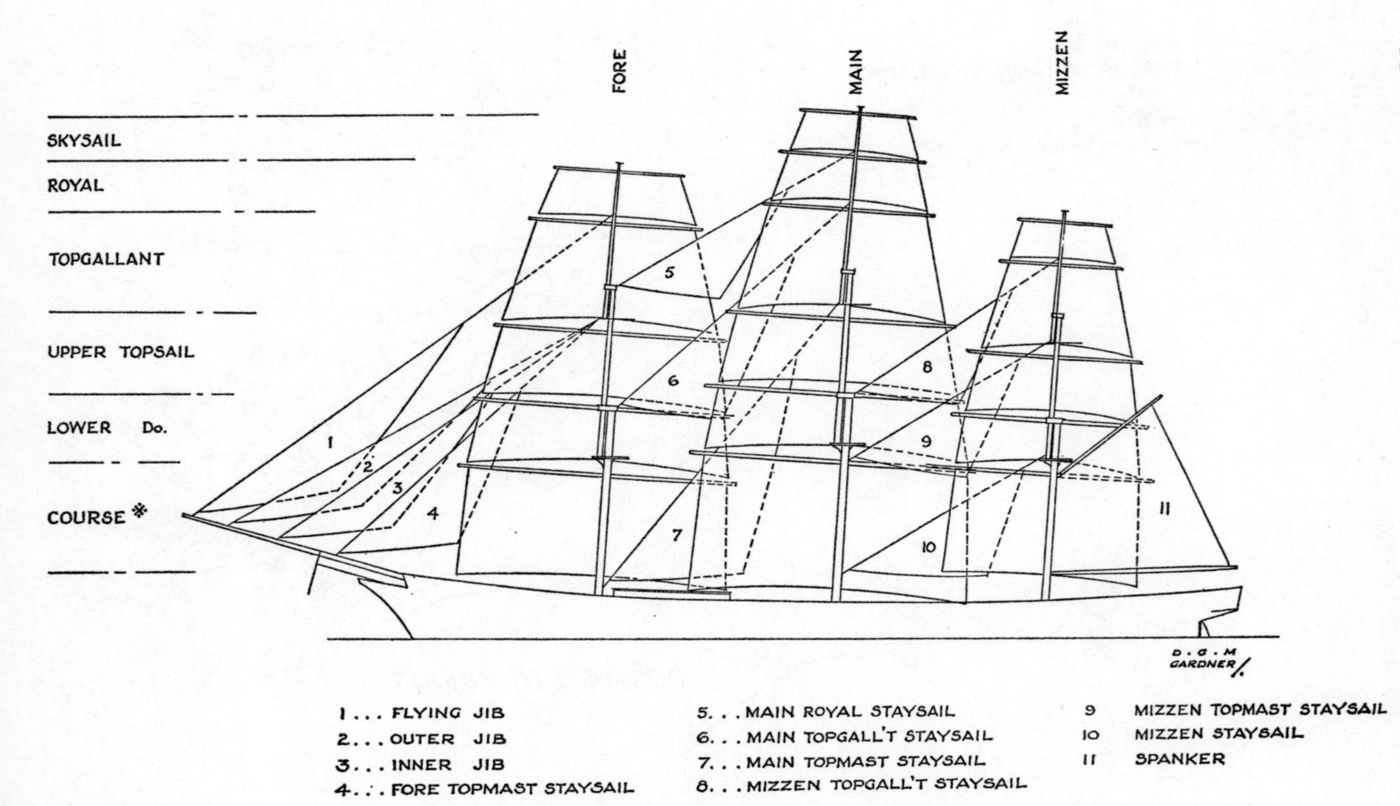

FULL-RIGGED SHIP

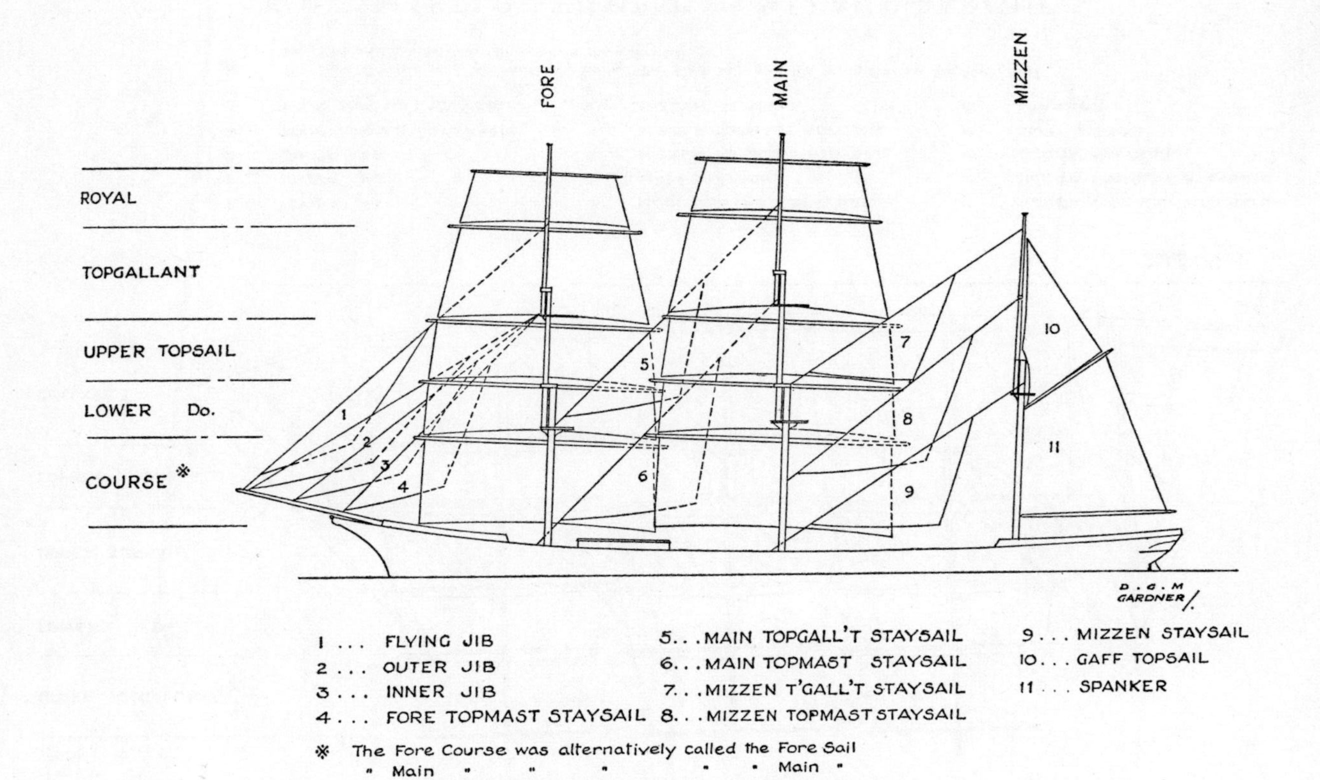

THREE-MASTED BARQUE

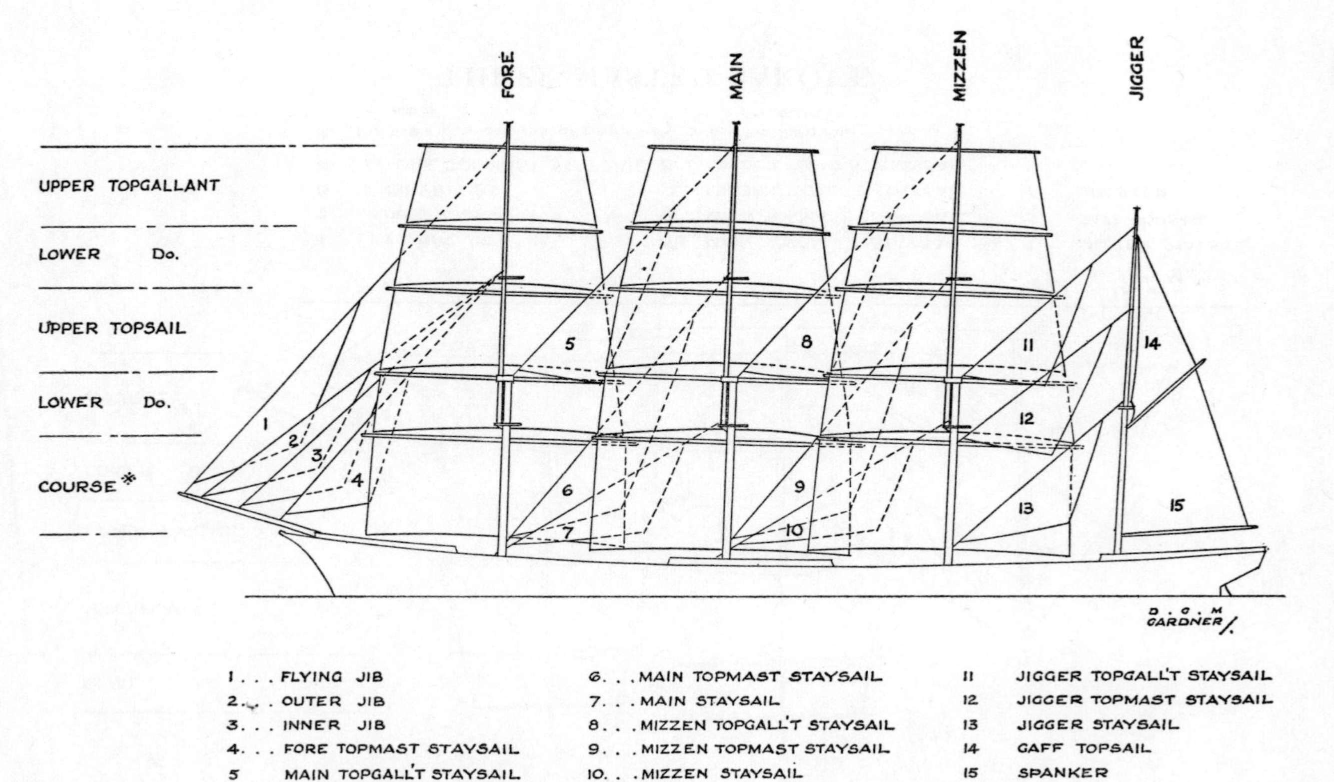

FOUR-MASTED STUMP TOPGALLANT BARQUE

Index